Reforming the Global Financial Architecture
Issues and Proposals

Edited by Yılmaz Akyüz

UNCTAD
Geneva

TWN
Third World Network
Penang, Malaysia

Zed Books
London & New York

Reforming the Global Financial Architecture: Issues and Proposals
is published for and on behalf of the United Nations

UNCTAD
United Nations Conference on Trade and Development
Palais des Nations
CH-1211 Geneva 10, Switzerland

Third World Network
228 Macalister Road
10400 Penang, Malaysia

Zed Books Ltd.
7 Cynthia Street
London, N1 9JF, UK
and Room 400, 175 Fifth Avenue
New York, NY 10010, USA

Distributed exclusively in the United States on behalf of Zed Books by
Palgrave
a division of St Martin's Press, LLC
175 Fifth Avenue
New York, NY 10010, USA.

Printed by Jutaprint
2 Solok Sungei Pinang 3, Sg. Pinang
11600 Penang, Malaysia.

ISBN   983 9747 70 3 (TWN)
ISBN   1 84277 154 X hb (Zed Books)
ISBN   1 84277 155 8 pb (Zed Books)

US CIP data is available from the Library of Congress.
British Cataloguing-in-Publication Data is available from the British Library.

NOTES

This book is based on the *Trade and Development Report (TDR), 2001*, Part Two, which was coordinated and edited by Yılmaz Akyüz. Chapters 1 and 4 were written by Yılmaz Akyüz, Chapter 2 by Andrew Cornford, and Chapter 3 jointly by Yılmaz Akyüz and Heiner Flassbeck. Comments and suggestions were received from Detlef Kotte, Richard Kozul-Wright and Jan Kregel of UNCTAD, as well as from B.L. Das, G. Helleiner, J.A. Ocampo and C. Raghavan; however, they are not responsible for any remaining errors or omissions.

The designations employed and the presentation of the material in this publication do not imply the expression of any opinion whatsoever on the part of the Secretariat of the United Nations concerning the legal status of any country, territory, city or area, or of its authorities, or concerning the delimitation of its frontiers or boundaries.

ABOUT THE AUTHORS

Yılmaz Akyüz is Director of the Division on Globalization and Development Strategies at the United Nations Conference on Trade and Development (UNCTAD). He is the principal author and head of the team which prepares UNCTAD's annual *Trade and Development Report*. He also serves as UNCTAD's coordinator of support to the Group of 24 at the IMF and World Bank on international monetary and financial issues. Previous to joining the UN system, he was Professor of Economics at various universities, including Ankara University, the Middle East Technical University in Turkey and the University of East Anglia in the United Kingdom. His teaching and research has focused on macroeconomics issues including finance, the international monetary system, economic growth and development. He has written widely on these topics.

Andrew Cornford, who received his BA from Cambridge University in 1964 and his Ph.D. from Oxford University in 1976, has worked at UNCTAD on financial and macroeconomic issues since 1977. During the Uruguay Round, as a member of the UNCTAD group which provided assistance to developing-country negotiators, he covered financial services. Since that time, much of his work has concerned financial regulation, a subject on which he has published several papers. His responsibilities also include the preparation of the commentary in the *Trade and Development Report* on international financial markets.

Heiner Flassbeck is a Senior Economist at UNCTAD. He was previously State Secretary (Vice Minister) at the German Federal Ministry of Finance and has served as Economic Adviser to the Government of Kazakhstan. Dr Flassbeck, whose areas of expertise include monetary issues, economic policy strategies and business cycle analysis, is also former Head of the Business Cycles Department at the German Institute for Economic Research and was a Visiting Fellow at MIT.

Contents

CHAPTER 3

EXCHANGE RATE REGIMES AND THE SCOPE FOR REGIONAL COOPERATION
Yılmaz Akyüz and Heiner Flassbeck

CHAPTER 4

CRISIS MANAGEMENT AND BURDEN SHARING
Yılmaz Akyüz

ABBREVIATIONS

APG	Asia/Pacific Group on Money Laundering
ASA	ASEAN Swap Arrangement
ASEAN	Association of South-East Asian Nations
BCBS	Basel Committee on Banking Supervision
BIS	Bank for International Settlements
CAC	collective action clause
CCL	Contingency Credit Line (IMF)
CFA	Communauté financiere africaine
CFATF	Caribbean Financial Action Task Force
CFR	(United States) Council on Foreign Relations
CFRTF	(United States) Council on Foreign Relations Task Force
CPLG	Core Principles Liaison Group (of BCBS)
CPSS	Committee on Payment Settlement Systems (of BIS)
EEC	European Economic Community
EMI	European Monetary Institute
EMS	European Monetary System
EMU	European Monetary Union
ERM	Exchange Rate Mechanism
EU	European Union
FASB	Financial Accounting Standards Board (United States)
FATF	Financial Action Task Force on Money Laundering
FDI	foreign direct investment
FLAR	Fondo Latinoamericano de Reservas
FSAP	Financial Sector Assessment Programme (IMF-World Bank)
FSF	Financial Stability Forum
GAAP	Generally Accepted Accounting Principles of the United States
GAB	(IMF's) General Arrangements to Borrow
GATS	General Agreement on Trade in Services
GATT	General Agreement on Tariffs and Trade
GDDS	General Data Dissemination System
GDP	gross domestic product
HKMA	Hong Kong Monetary Authority
HLI	highly leveraged institution
IAIS	International Association of Insurance Supervisors
IASC	International Accounting Standards Committee
IFAC	International Federation of Accountants

IFAD	International Fund for Agricultural Development
IFIC	International Financial Institutions Commission
IIF	Institute for International Finance
IMF	International Monetary Fund
IMFC	International Monetary and Financial Committee
IOSCO	International Organization of Securities Commissions
LTCM	Long Term Capital Management
NIE	newly industrializing economy
OECD	Organization for Economic Cooperation and Development
OFC	offshore financial centre
SDDS	Special Data Dissemination Standard
SDR	special drawing right
SRF	Supplemental Reserve Facility (of IMF)
SWIFT	Society for Worldwide Inter-Bank Financial Telecommunications
TDR	Trade and Development Report
UDROP	universal debt rollover option with a penalty
UNCTAD	United Nations Conference on Trade and Development
UNCTC	United Nations Centre on Transnational Corporations
WTO	World Trade Organization

Preface

BETWEEN the myopia of global markets and the myth of global government, multilateral rules and institutions can help reduce market volatility and prevent mutually incompatible policy responses to economic shocks. For the architects of the post-war multilateral system who gathered at Bretton Woods, history had taught that financial markets were a particularly fecund source of instability and shocks, and that control over international capital flows was a precondition for currency stability, the revival of trade and economic growth and the achievement of full employment.

The breakdown of the Bretton Woods system in the early 1970s initiated a period of financial and economic uncertainty and instability that shares at least some of the characteristics of the inter-war period. Various initiatives have been pursued in different forums in the hope of finding a system of governance compatible with flexible exchange rates and large-scale private capital flows. The history of these initiatives can point to some successes but has, by and large, proved unsatisfactory, in part because they have been premised on keeping separate the problems facing developed and developing countries within the multilateral financial arrangements.

When the Asian financial crisis erupted, it seemed that all that would change. The virulence of the economic forces unleashed after the collapse of the Thai baht in July 1997, and among countries with track records of good governance and macroeconomic discipline, seemed to confirm the systemic nature and global reach of currency and financial crises. But despite the initial emphasis of some policy-makers in the leading industrial economies on the need for systemic reform, moves in that direction have subsequently stalled. Instead of establishing institutions and mechanisms at the international level to reduce the likelihood of such crises and better manage them when they do occur, there has been a very one-sided emphasis on reforming domestic institutions and policies in developing countries.

Efforts in the past few years have focused on measures designed to discipline debtors and provide costly self-defence mechanisms. Countries have been urged to better manage risk by adopting strict financial standards, improving transparency, adopting appropriate exchange rate regimes, carrying large amounts of reserves, and making voluntary arrangements with private creditors to involve them in crisis resolution. While some of these reforms undoubtedly have their merits, they presume that the cause of crises rests primarily with policy and institutional weaknesses in the debtor countries and accordingly place the onus of responsibility for reform firmly on their shoulders. By contrast, little attention is given to the role played by institutions and policies in creditor countries in triggering international financial crises.

* * * *

Proposals for new international institutions explicitly designed to regulate and stabilize international capital flows have been summarily dismissed by critics as the work of mavericks lacking in political sense and technical judgement. The preferred line of reform has sought to establish various codes and standards to help strengthen domestic financial systems in debtor countries, enhance their macroeconomic and financial policy formulation, and improve the collection and disclosure of information. The Bretton Woods institutions, the Basel-based bodies and the Financial Stability Forum have already made a series of proposals along these lines.

Such measures can bring self-evident benefits, but they can be properly assessed only as part of an evolutionary process of stabilizing global financial markets. Of more immediate concern to developing countries is the fact that what has been proposed so far under the heading of codes and standards embodies the view that the main problems lie in countries receiving capital flows, but entails neither a fundamental change in policies and practices in the source countries nor improvement in the transparency and regulation of currently unregulated cross-border financial operations. And despite the emphasis on their voluntary adoption, there is the danger that incentives and sanctions linked to standard-setting will become features of IMF surveillance and conditionality, compliance with which would place a further heavy burden on the administrative capacities of many countries.

Because much of the impetus to improve codes and standards assumes their introduction into a stable and predictable global financial system, such measures offer little in the way of immediate protection for developing countries against supply-driven fluctuations in international capital flows, which are strongly influenced by policies and monetary conditions in the major industrial countries. Almost all major crises in emerging markets have been connected with shifts in exchange rates and monetary policy in those countries. The root of this problem lies, in large part, in the failure to establish a stable system of exchange rates after the breakdown of the Bretton Woods arrangements. The expectation then was that floating among the main reserve currencies would automatically bring about orderly balance-of-payments adjustments, increased exchange-rate stability and greater macroeconomic policy autonomy. This has not happened. But while the damage inflicted by disorderly exchange-rate behaviour has been limited for the G-3 (major reserve currency) economies, this has not been the case for debtor developing countries, which depend more heavily on trade and whose borrowing profile exposes them to greater currency risk.

Despite the broad consensus that the Bretton Woods institutions should get back to what they do best, the discussion on reforming the international financial and monetary system has so far avoided serious mention of how the IMF might help rebuild a stable exchange rate system among the G-3 currencies. Proposals for securing greater stability through coordinated intervention and macroeconomic policy action, including formally established target zones, have been brushed aside, and discussions have concentrated on the pros and cons for developing countries of fixed or floating exchange-rate regimes and the macroeconomic policies consistent with one or the other of these "corner solutions". This ignores the mounting evidence that developing countries cannot unilaterally ensure appropriate alignment and stability of their exchange rates as long as major reserve currencies are subject to frequent gyrations and misalignments and international capital flows to large swings beyond the control of recipient countries.

* * * *

With little progress on how best to prevent financial crises, attention has increasingly turned to how best to limit their damage through faster and more effective responses once they do occur. So far, large bailout packages have been the preferred option, in most creditor and debtor countries alike, but they are becoming increasingly problematic. Not only do they create moral hazard for lenders but also they shift the burden of the crisis firmly onto taxpayers in debtor countries. Moreover, the approach is running into political opposition in creditor countries as crises become more frequent and extensive and the funds required get larger.

Thus, ways and means have been sought to redress the balance of burden-sharing between official and private creditors, as well as between debtors and creditors, by involving private creditors in crisis management and resolution. The issue is a contentious one. While the international community has come to recognize that market discipline will only work if creditors bear the consequences of the risks they take, it has been unable to reach agreement on how to bring this about.

For some time now the UNCTAD secretariat has been advocating a temporary standstill on debt payments during crisis situations to prevent asset grabbing by creditors, combined with lending into arrears to ensure that debtors have access to working capital. Although such procedures do not need full-fledged international bankruptcy procedures, they do need effective mandatory backing at the international level. Such backing has met with strong opposition from some of the major economic powers and market participants, who favour voluntary arrangements between debtors and creditors. Governments in some debtor countries have also been reluctant to back this proposal for fear of impairing their access to international capital markets. However, voluntary arrangements, while potentially helpful in debt restructuring, are unlikely to halt asset grab races. Again, the evidence from recent settlements suggests that without statutory protection for debtors the balance of power will continue to weigh heavily in favour of creditors.

A credible strategy for involving the private sector in crisis management and resolution should combine mandatory temporary standstills with strict limits on access to IMF resources. A first step in this direction would be the design of explicit guidelines under the IMF's Articles of Agreement allowing a stay on creditor litigation in order to provide statutory protection for debtors imposing temporary standstills. On the other hand, since the main objective of large-scale crisis or contingency lending would be to keep debtors current on their obligations to creditors, it would be difficult to ensure private sector involvement without limiting access to IMF financing. There is indeed growing agreement on the need to limit crisis lending. In setting such limits, it must be recognized that current IMF quotas have lagged far behind the growth of global output, trade and financial flows, and may not provide appropriate yardsticks to evaluate the desirable limits to normal access. However, the current approach still appears to favour large-scale packages for countries considered to present systemic risks, while other countries would face access limits and be encouraged to default in order to involve their private lenders in the resolution of their financial difficulties.

* * * *

The above are not the only changes needed in the mandates and policies of the Bretton Woods institutions. Over the past two decades, the unwillingness of the advanced countries to defer to the IMF on contentious monetary and financial matters which directly affect their own interests has meant that the Fund's surveillance of the policies of the most important players in the global system has lost any real purpose. Instead, there has been an intensification of surveillance of developing countries, which has now been extended to include financial-sector issues, consistent with the diagnosis that the main flaws are to be found in debtor countries.

One result has been the expansion of conditionalities attached to IMF lending to countries facing actual or potential crisis. This has given rise to serious concerns about undermining sovereign responsibility, even as the effectiveness of IMF surveillance is increasingly questioned. These concerns increased in the aftermath of the East Asian crisis, when excessive conditionalities led to policy responses which intensified the crisis. As a result, there have been calls, including within the International Monetary and Financial Committee, for the streamlining and refocusing of surveillance in line with the Fund's core competence in macroeconomic policy and related reforms. However, the recent financial difficulties in Turkey and Argentina illustrate the reluctance to break with the past practice of attaching wide-ranging policy recommendations to any IMF-negotiated loan package.

With swings in exchange rates and monetary policies in the major industrial economies acting as a catalyst for crises elsewhere in the world economy, a priority of the reform process must be strengthening surveillance mechanisms to achieve a minimum degree of coherence among the macroeconomic policies of those countries. In view of the asymmetries in existing practices, one way forward might be to link surveillance procedures to a mechanism analogous to that used for settling disputes in international trade, where disagreements over the impact of macroeconomic and financial policies could be taken up and their resolution sought.

More radical reform proposals put forward so far have sought to build on the consensus that the Fund should provide international liquidity not only to countries facing current-account difficulties but also to those facing capital-account crises. According to the Meltzer Commission, the time has come to make the Fund an international lender of last resort for any economy able to meet a series of *ex ante* conditions for solvency. This proposal raises two major concerns. On the one hand, it is likely to result in much larger packages than existing crisis lending, with attendant moral-hazard problems for lenders and no incentive for bailing in the private sector. On the other hand, a radical shift in IMF lending to short-term capital-account financing would deny access to multilateral financing to all those developing countries considered systemically unimportant. These proposals place inordinate faith in market forces both to resolve financial crises and to provide finance for development.

One of the original objectives of the IMF was to provide short-term financing to countries facing current-account problems due to temporary shocks and disturbances so as to ensure an orderly adjustment process. Experience continues to show that financial markets often fail to meet such needs, as they tend to be pro-cyclical. Given the increased instability of the external trading and financial environment of developing countries, an effective reform of the Bretton Woods institutions should seek to improve, not eliminate, counter-cyclical and emergency financing for trade and other current transactions.

* * * *

There are certainly a number of conceptual and technical difficulties in designing reasonably effective global mechanisms for achieving currency and financial stability. Such difficulties are familiar from the design of national systems. At the international level, there are additional political problems associated with striking the right balance between multilateral disciplines and national sovereignty. Indeed, political constraints and conflicts appear to be the main reason why the international community has not been able to achieve significant progress in setting up effective global arrangements for the prevention and management of financial crises. In particular, the process has been driven by the interests of the major creditor countries, which hold most of the power in the multilateral financial institutions, as well as in bodies set up more recently with the explicit intention of reforming the international financial architecture. As a result, many of the issues of crucial importance to developing countries have been excluded from the reform agenda.

If reforms to the existing financial structures are to be credible, they must provide for much greater collective influence from developing countries and embody a genuine spirit of cooperation among all countries. This will require a major reformulation of the reform agenda. It will also require careful examination of the representation in the existing multilateral financial institutions and of their decision-making practices.

But it is equally important that developing countries themselves reach a consensus on how they want the reform process to move forward. While this consensus is lacking on several issues of the reform agenda, there are many commonly shared objectives, including: more balanced and symmetrical treatment of debtors and creditors regarding standards, codes, transparency and regulation; more stable exchange rates; more symmetrical surveillance; less intrusive conditionality; and above all, multilateral institutions and processes that are more democratic and participatory. Effective reform of the international monetary and financial system will ultimately depend on the willingness of developing countries to organize their efforts around such common objectives, and on acceptance by developed countries that accommodating these objectives will be an essential part of building a more inclusive system of global economic governance.

In the absence of collective arrangements for a stable international financial system, developing countries should avoid commitments which restrict their policy autonomy with respect to dealing with financial instability. Interest is now growing in regional arrangements to provide collective defence mechanisms against systemic failures and instability, and regional currencies are increasingly seen as viable alternatives to dollarization. The European experience has also been held up as a model for regional arrangements, including in areas such as intraregional currency bands, intervention mechanisms, regimes for capital movements, payments support and regional lender-of-last-resort facilities. Such arrangements among developing countries probably require the inclusion of a major reserve-currency country willing and able to assume a key role for this purpose. In this respect, recent initiatives in Asia, involving developing countries and Japan, could constitute an important step towards closer regional monetary integration.

Rubens Ricupero
Secretary-General of UNCTAD

Chapter 1

Towards Reform of the International Financial Architecture: Which Way Forward?

Yılmaz Akyüz

A. INTRODUCTION

THE increased frequency and virulence of international currency and financial crises, involving even countries with a record of good governance and macroeconomic discipline, suggests that instability is global and systemic. Although there is room to improve national policies and institutions, that alone would not be sufficient to deal with the problem, particularly in developing countries, where the potential threat posed by inherently unstable capital flows is much greater. A strengthening of institutions and arrangements at the international level is essential if the threat of such crises is to be reduced and if they are to be better managed whenever they do occur. Yet, despite growing agreement on the global and systemic nature of financial instability, the international community has so far been unable to achieve significant progress in establishing effective global arrangements that address the main concerns of developing countries.

In the aftermath of the Asian crisis a number of proposals have been made by governments, international organizations, academia and market participants for the reform of the international financial architecture.[1] They cover broadly four areas: global rules and institutions governing international capital flows; the exchange rate system; orderly workouts for international debt; and the reform of the International Monetary Fund (IMF), with special reference to surveillance, conditionality, the provision of international liquidity, and its potential function as lender of last resort. Implementation of any of these

---

[1] For a survey of these proposals, see *TDR 1998* (Part One, chap. IV); Akyüz (2000); and Rogoff (1999).

proposals would entail the creation of new international institutions and mechanisms as well as reform of the existing ones. Some of these proposals have been discussed in the IMF itself, as well as in other international financial institutions, such as the Bank for International Settlements (BIS) and the newly-established Financial Stability Forum (FSF), and also among the governments of the G-7 (Group of Seven leading industrial countries). While certain initiatives have been taken as a result, the reform process, rather than focusing on international action to address systemic instability and risks, has placed emphasis on what should be done by national institutions and mechanisms. Even in this regard it has failed to adopt an even-handed approach between debtors and creditors. Efforts have concentrated on disciplining debtors, setting guidelines and standards for major areas of national policy, principally in debtor countries, and providing incentives and sanctions for their implementation. Debtor countries have been urged to better manage risk by adopting strict financial standards and regulations, carrying adequate amounts of international reserves, establishing contingent credit lines and making contractual arrangements with private creditors so as to involve them in crisis resolution. The international financial system has continued to be organized around the principle of *laissez-faire, laissez-passer,* and developing countries are advised to adhere to the objective of an open capital account and convertibility, and to resort to controls over capital flows only as an exceptional and temporary measure. All this has extended the global reach of financial markets without a corresponding strengthening of global institutions.

The failure to achieve greater progress is, to a considerable extent, political in nature. The proposals referred to above have often run into conflict with the interests of creditors. But governments in some debtor countries also oppose reform measures that would have the effect of lowering the volume of capital inflows and/or raising their cost, even when such measures could be expected to reduce instability and the frequency of emerging-market crises. Many observers have been quick to dismiss such proposals as not only politically unrealistic but also technically impossible. However, as long as systemic failure continues to threaten global welfare, resistance to more fundamental reform of the international financial architecture must be overcome:

It is easy to fall into the trap of thinking that big institutional changes are unrealistic or infeasible, especially in the United States where macroeconomic policy institutions have generally evolved only slowly for the past few decades. Not so long ago, the prospects for a single European currency seemed no more likely than those for the breakup of the Soviet empire or the reunification of Germany. Perhaps large institutional changes only seem impossible until they happen – at which point they seem foreordained. Even if none of the large-scale plans is feasible in the present world political environment, after another crisis or two, the impossible may start seeming realistic. (Rogoff, 1999: 28)

This book reviews the main initiatives undertaken so far in the reform of the international financial architecture, and the advice given to developing countries in some key policy areas, such as structural reforms and exchange rate policy, for the prevention and management of instability and crises. The discussion follows from an earlier analysis, made in the United Nations Conference on Trade and Development's (UNCTAD) *Trade and Development Report 1998 (TDR 1998)*, and concentrates on more recent developments. This chapter provides an overview of the issues, comparing briefly what has so far been achieved with the kind of measures proposed in order to address systemic failures and global instability. Chapter 2 reviews recent initiatives regarding global standards and regulation, while Chapter 3 discusses whether developing countries can both keep an open capital account and avoid currency instability and misalignments by choosing appropriate exchange rate regimes, despite persistent misalignments and gyrations of the three major reserve currencies and large swings in international capital flows. It also assesses the scope for regional cooperation for establishing collective defence mechanisms against financial instability, drawing on the European Union experience. Chapter 4 takes up the question of the management of financial crises and burden sharing, and discusses the current state of play in two crucial areas, namely the provision of international liquidity and the involvement of the private sector in crisis management and resolution.

B. THE GOVERNANCE OF INTERNATIONAL CAPITAL FLOWS

As the Second World War drew to an end, a set of organizations was envisaged which would deal with exchange rates and international payments, the reconstruction and rehabilitation of war damaged economies, and international trade and investment. The institutions established to handle these issues were the IMF, the World Bank and the General Agreement on Tariffs and Trade (GATT). However, international capital movements did not fall within their purview. The original structure did not include a global regime for capital movements in large part because it was considered that capital mobility was not compatible with currency stability and expansion of trade and employment. However, no such regime was established even after the breakdown of the Bretton Woods arrangements, despite the growing importance of private capital flows (Akyüz and Cornford, 1999: 1-7).

The only global regime applying to cross-border monetary transactions was that of the IMF, but the most important obligations in its Articles of Agreement relate to current and not capital transactions. Concerning the latter, Article IV states that one of the essential purposes of the international monetary system is to provide a framework facilitating the exchange of capital among countries, a statement which is included among general obligations regarding exchange arrangements. The more specific references to capital transfers, in Article VI, permit recourse to capital controls so long as they do not restrict payments for current transactions, and actually give the Fund the authority to request a member country to impose controls to prevent the use of funds from its General Resources Account to finance a large or sustained capital outflow. The only recent initiative regarding the global regime is the attempt to include capital convertibility among the objectives of the IMF.

The BIS was originally set up as a forum for a small number of countries to deal with only certain aspects of international capital flows.[2] Since the 1970s it has provided secretariat support for a number of bodies established to reduce or manage the risks in cross-border banking transactions. These bodies are not responsible for setting rules for international capital movements as such. Their work is aimed at reaching agreements on standards to be applied by national authorities for strengthening the defences of financial firms, both individually and in the aggregate against destabilization due to cross-border transactions and risk exposures.

The increased frequency of financial crises, together with the increasingly global character of financial markets, has prompted both analysts and practitioners to formulate proposals for the creation of a number of international institutions explicitly designed to regulate and stabilize international capital flows. One such proposal is for the creation of a global mega-agency for financial regulation and supervision, or World Financial Authority, with responsibility for setting regulatory standards for all financial enterprises, offshore as well as onshore (Eatwell and Taylor, 1998; 2000). Another proposal is to establish a Board of Overseers of Major International Institutions and Markets, with wide-ranging powers for setting standards and for the oversight and regulation of commercial banking, securities business and insurance.[3] Yet another proposal, which focuses on stabilizing international bank lending, is for the establishment of an International Credit Insurance Corporation designed to reduce the likelihood of excessive credit expansion (Soros, 1998).

These proposals are based on two arguments. The first is that, since financial businesses are becoming increasingly interrelated and operate across borders, their regulation and supervision should also be

---

[2] For a useful summary of the history, structure, functions and legal status of the BIS, see Edwards (1985: 52-63). Until recently the principal shareholders of the BIS were 28 predominantly West European central banks, with those of Belgium, France, Germany, Italy and United Kingdom holding over 50 per cent of the votes. The United States Federal Reserve participates in meetings and committees linked to the BIS without being a shareholder. More recently the BIS invited additional central banks from emerging markets to become shareholders.

[3] Kaufman (1992: 57); and "Preventing the next global financial crisis", *Washington Post*, 28 January 2001, A.17. See also speaking notes by H. Kaufman for the Extraordinary Ministerial Meeting of the Group of 24, Caracas, February 1998.

Certainly, given the degree of global interdependence, a stable system of exchange rates and payments positions calls for a minimum degree of coherence among the macroeconomic policies of major industrial countries. But the existing modalities of multilateral surveillance do not include ways of attaining such coherence or dealing with unidirectional impulses resulting from changes in the monetary and exchange rate policies of the United States and other major industrial countries. In this respect governance in macroeconomic and financial policies lacks the kind of multilateral disciplines that exist for international trade.

One proposal to attain stable and properly aligned exchange rates is through the introduction of target zones among the three major currencies together with a commitment by the countries to defend such zones through coordinated intervention and macroeconomic policy action.[5] It is felt that such a commitment would secure the policy coherence needed for exchange rate stability without undermining growth and could alter the behaviour of currency markets, which, in turn, would reduce the need for intervention. Such an arrangement could be institutionalized and placed under IMF surveillance.

A more radical proposal is to do away with exchange rates and adopt a single world currency, to be issued by a World Monetary Authority which could also act as a lender of last resort. There has been growing interest in such an arrangement since the introduction of the euro and the recurrent currency crises in emerging markets. However, it is generally felt that the present extent of economic convergence and depth of global integration fall far short of what would be required for such an arrangement to operate effectively (Rogoff, 1999: 33-34).

In any event, it is interesting to note that the exchange rate system has hardly figured on the agenda for the reform of the international financial architecture. The report by the then Acting Managing Director of the IMF to the International Monetary and Financial Committee (IMF, 2000) recognized the difficult choice faced by most countries between maintaining, on the one hand, truly flexible rates and, on the other, hard pegs. Referring to the three major currencies, the report pointed to "large misalignments and volatility" in their exchange rates as a cause for concern, particularly for small, open commodity-

---

[5]   This proposal was first made in Williamson (1983).

exporting countries. However, it did not discuss any initiatives that might be taken by the international community in this respect, implying that the matter could only be sorted out between the United States, Japan and the EU (see also Culpeper, 2000: 15).

Indeed, as noted in Chapter 3, discussions on exchange rates have concentrated on the kind of regimes that developing countries would need to adopt in order to attain greater stability. The mainstream advice is to choose between free floating or locking into a reserve currency through currency boards or dollarization (the "hard" pegs), thus opting for one of the two "corner" solutions, as opposed to intermediate regimes of adjustable or soft pegs. Increasingly questions are being raised as to whether the existence of so many independent currencies makes sense in a closely integrated global financial system.

However, much of this is a false debate. Whichever option is chosen, it will not be able to ensure appropriate alignment and stability of exchange rates in developing countries as long as major reserve currencies themselves are so unstable and misaligned, and international capital flows are volatile and beyond the control of recipient countries. Moreover, such conditions create inconsistencies within the developing world in attaining orderly exchange rates. Briefly put, there is no satisfactory unilateral solution to exchange rate instability and misalignments in emerging markets, particularly under free capital movements.

Since global arrangements for a stable system are not on the immediate agenda, the question arises as to whether regional mechanisms could provide a way out. Indeed, there is now a growing interest in East Asia and some countries of South America in regionalization (as opposed to dollarization) as a means of providing a collective defence mechanism against systemic failures and instability. The EU experience holds useful lessons in this respect, including the institutional arrangements for the maintenance and adjustment of intraregional currency bands, intervention mechanisms, regimes for capital movements, and various facilities designed to provide payments support to individual countries and regional lender-of-last-resort services. However, applying this experience to arrangements among developing countries poses certain difficulties, particularly with respect to the exchange rate regime to be pursued *vis-a-vis* reserve currencies and access to international liquidity, issues of special importance under

tively high degree of dependence on financial inflows, are opposed to both mandatory standstills and the inclusion of collective action clauses in bond contracts for fear that their access to international financial markets would be impaired.

The discussions in the IMF Executive Board on this issue emphasized the catalytic role of the Fund in involving the private sector and that, if the latter did not respond, the debtor country should seek agreement with its creditors on a voluntary standstill. The Board recognized that, "in extreme circumstances, if it is not possible to reach agreement on a voluntary standstill, members may find it necessary, as a last resort, to impose one unilaterally". However, there is no agreement over empowering the IMF, through an amendment of its Articles of Agreement, to impose a stay on creditor litigation in order to provide statutory protection to debtors imposing temporary standstills. While it is generally accepted that the Fund may signal its acceptance of a unilateral standstill by lending into arrears, no explicit guidelines have been established on when and how such support would be provided, thus leaving considerable discretion to the Fund and its major shareholders regarding the modalities of its intervention in financial crises in emerging markets.

As in other areas, the reform process has thus been unable to establish an appropriate international framework for involving the private sector in the management and resolution of financial crises, passing the buck again to debtor countries. True enough, contractual arrangements, such as collective action clauses in bond contracts and call options in interbank credit lines, can provide considerable relief for countries facing debt servicing difficulties, and the misgivings that such arrangements may impede access to capital markets may be misplaced. But these are not matters for consideration in the reform of the international financial architecture, unless global mechanisms are introduced to facilitate such arrangements. There is also resistance to introducing automatic rollover and collective action clauses in international debt contracts based on an international mandate. Furthermore, certain features of external debt of developing countries, including wide dispersion of creditors and debtors and the existence of a large variety of debt contracts, governed by different laws, render it extremely difficult to rely on voluntary mechanisms for securing rapid debt standstills and rollovers. Without a statutory protection of debtors, negotiations with creditors for restructuring loans cannot be expected to result in equitable burden sharing. Indeed, in recent examples of negotiated settlements the creditors have not borne the consequences of the risk they had taken; rather, they have forced the developing-country governments to assume responsibility for the private debt and accept a simple maturity extension at penalty rates.

E.   REFORM OF THE IMF

Naturally, reforms and recent initiatives in the areas discussed above generally imply significant changes in the mandate and policies of the IMF, particularly with respect to bilateral and multilateral surveillance, conditionality and the provision of international liquidity. As noted above, the Fund is closely involved in setting codes and standards for macroeconomic and financial policies and monitoring compliance, and effective multilateral surveillance is a prerequisite for a stable system of exchange rates. Private sector involvement in crisis management and resolution also crucially depends on IMF lending policies, as well as on its support and sanctioning of standstills and capital and exchange controls. Consequently, the reform of the international financial architecture presupposes a reform of the IMF.

1.   Surveillance and conditionality

As discussed in *TDR 1998*, asymmetries in IMF surveillance, in the aftermath of the East Asian crisis, along with excessive conditionality attached to IMF lending, were widely considered to be two of the principal areas deserving attention in the reform of the international financial architecture. However, the recent approach to reform has resulted in increased asymmetries in surveillance and in enhanced conditionality, since it has focused primarily on policy and institutional shortcomings in debtor countries.

As already noted, surveillance has not been successful in ensuring stable and appropriately aligned exchange rates among the three major reserve currencies. Nor has it been able to protect weaker and smaller economies against adverse impulses originating from monetary and financial policies in the major industrial countries. It is true that the need for stronger IMF surveillance in response to conditions produced by greater global financial integration and recurrent crises was recognized by the Interim Committee in April 1998, when it agreed that the Fund "should intensify its surveillance of financial sector issues and capital flows, giving particular attention to policy interdependence and risks of contagion, and ensure that it is fully aware of market views and perspectives" (IMF Interim Committee Communiqué of 16 April 1998). However, despite the reference to interdependence and contagion, these proposals have not so far been effectively extended to cover weaknesses arising from the lack of balance in existing procedures.

Rather, there has been an intensification of IMF surveillance and conditionality as a result of their extension to financial sector issues in debtor countries, in accordance with the diagnosis that this is where the main problem lies. As noted above, new codes and standards are likely to result in enhanced conditionality, particularly for the use of new facilities, including contingency financing, for overcoming financial crises. Quite apart from whether the result could be unnecessary interference with the proper jurisdiction of a sovereign government, as some commentators believed it was in the Republic of Korea (Feldstein, 1998), there is also the potential problem that the type of measures and institutions promoted may not be the appropriate ones:

> An unappreciated irony in this is that conditionality on develop-
> ing countries is being ratcheted up at precisely the moment when
> our comprehension of how the world economy works and what
> small countries need to do to prosper within it has been revealed
> to be sorely lacking. (Rodrik, 1999: 2)

The International Monetary and Financial Committee (IMFC, formerly the Interim Committee), recognizing the need to streamline IMF conditionality, has urged "the Executive Board to take forward its review of all aspects of policy conditionality associated with Fund financing in order to ensure that, while not weakening that conditionality, it focuses on the most essential issues".[6] For his part, the Fund's

---

[6] Communiqué of the International Monetary and Financial Committee of the Board of Governors of the International Monetary Fund, 24 September 2000, Washington, DC: para. 11.

Managing Director, Horst Köhler, has likewise concluded that:

> To strengthen its efficiency and legitimacy, the Fund needs to refocus. The Fund's focus must clearly be to promote macroeconomic stability as an essential condition for sustained growth. To pursue this objective, the Fund has to concentrate on fostering sound monetary, fiscal and exchange rate policies, along with their institutional underpinning and closely related structural reforms. ... I trust that ownership is promoted when the Fund's conditionality focuses in content and timing predominantly on what is crucial for the achievement of macroeconomic stability and growth. Less can be more if it helps to break the ground for sustained process of adjustment and growth.[7]

Perhaps it is too early to judge how far in practice this refocusing has been pursued, but it is notable that the recent Fund programmes in Turkey and Argentina show no significant tendency to depart from past practice *(TDR 2001,* chap. II, boxes 2.1 and 2.2). They stipulate a wide range of policy actions not only in the purview of other international organizations, such as the World Trade Organization (WTO) and the development banks, but also of national economic and social development strategies, including actions relating to privatization and deregulation, agricultural support, social security and pension systems, industrial and competition policy, and trade policy.

2. Liquidity provision and lender-of-last-resort financing

The other major area of reform concerns the provision of adequate liquidity. A consensus has emerged over the past decade that the Fund should provide international liquidity not only to countries facing payments difficulties on current account but also to those facing crises on capital account. Two main facilities have been established for this purpose: a Supplemental Reserve Facility (SRF) for countries already facing payments difficulties, and a Contingency Credit Line (CCL) to provide a precautionary line of defence against international

---

[7] Horst Köhler, Address to the Board of Governors, Fifty-fifth Annual Meeting, Prague, 26 September 2000.

financial contagion (see Chapter 4, box 6). While there are difficulties regarding the terms and conditions attached to such facilities, the real issue is whether and to what extent provision of such financing conflicts with, or complements the objective of, involving private creditors and investors in the management and resolution of emerging-market crises.

In several debtor countries, governments appear to favour unlimited liquidity support, regardless of the terms and conditions and the burden that may eventually be placed on the country's taxpayers by international rescue operations. This attitude is consistent with their aversion to imposing temporary payments standstills and capital and exchange controls at times of crisis. On the other hand, while there is no consensus in the IMF Board on mandatory arrangements for involving the private sector, there is now a growing emphasis on making official assistance conditional on private sector participation. However, no formal limits have been set for access to Fund resources beyond which such participation would be required. As discussed in Chapter 4, absence of explicit access limits as well as of mandatory standstill mechanisms may render it extremely difficult to secure private sector involvement, forcing the Fund to engage in large-scale interventions.

Indeed, since the main objective of large-scale contingency or crisis financing would be to allow debtor countries to remain current on payments to their creditors, it is difficult to see how this could be reconciled with a meaningful private sector involvement in crisis resolution and burden sharing. Consequently, a credible and effective strategy for involving the private sector should combine temporary standstills with strict limits on access to Fund resources. While there is growing agreement on the need to limit crisis lending, it is also suggested that there may be a need for exceptionally large contingency financing when the crisis appears to be "systemic". In practice, such an approach could result in differentiation among debtor countries: those for which the crisis is considered "systemic" would be eligible for considerable liquidity support without any prior condition for private sector participation, as in recent operations in Argentina and Turkey; those where the crisis is not so considered would face strict limits and would be encouraged to involve the private sector through default, as seems to have been the case for Ecuador and Pakistan.

There are proposals to go further and allow the IMF to act as, or to transform that institution into, an international lender of last resort for emerging markets. Proposals of this nature have been put forward by the Deputy Managing Director of the Fund (Fischer, 1999) and, in the broader context of reforming the international financial institutions, by the International Financial Institutions Advisory Commission (Meltzer Commission). Indeed, the idea has received much greater sympathy than any other proposal for institutional changes at the global level, from among people with sharply different views about the reform of the IMF and situated at opposite ends of the political spectrum, although certain aspects of the Meltzer Commission's recommendations are highly contentious.[8] The key suggestion is that countries meeting certain *ex ante* conditions for solvency should be eligible for lender-of-last-resort financing. In the proposal by the Meltzer Commission, access to liquidity would be automatic for countries meeting *a priori* requirements, and no additional conditionality or negotiations would be required. Lending would be limited to a maximum of one year's tax revenue of the borrowing country. This could result in far greater packages than any crisis lending by the IMF so far. The problem of moral hazard would be tackled by conditionality rather than by tighter limits on lending. By contrast, the report does not make any recommendation for involving the private sector, except to suggest that, for the time being, the matter should be left to negotiations between debtors and creditors.

Arrangements of this nature would, however, compound certain problems encountered in the current practice regarding IMF bailouts. Without discretion to create its own liquidity, the Fund would have to rely on major industrial countries to secure the funds needed for such operations. In such circumstances it is highly questionable whether it would really be able to act as an impartial lender of last resort, analogous to a national central bank, since its decisions and resources would depend on the consent of its major shareholders, who are typically creditors of those countries experiencing external financial

---

[8] See, for example, Wolf (2000); Eichengreen and Portes (2000); Summers (2000), and also L.H. Summers' Testimony before the Banking Committee of the House of Representatives, 23 March 2000; and Goldstein (2000). For similar proposals, see the references in Rogoff (1999).

difficulties. This problem could be partly overcome by authorizing the Fund to issue permanent or reversible special drawing rights (SDRs), but attributing such a key role to the SDR would face strong opposition from the same source.

Furthermore, there are also political and technical difficulties regarding the terms of access to such a facility. Financing by a genuine international lender of last resort, which would be unlimited and unconditional except for penalty rates, would require very tight global supervision over borrowers to ensure their solvency, which it would not be easy to reconcile with national sovereignty. Nor would prequalification be compatible with the practice of "constructive ambiguity" that all modern national lenders of resort are said to follow.[9] It would also require the IMF to act as a *de facto* credit-rating agency. However, it is very difficult to establish generally agreed standards for solvency, and assessments of a given set of economic indicators can vary considerably, as evidenced by differences among private rating agencies (Akyüz and Cornford, 1999: 48). Disagreements in this respect between the developing countries concerned and the Fund staff could lead the countries to opt out and seek alternative arrangements, thereby reducing the effectiveness of the proposed mechanism. Moreover, since it would be necessary constantly to monitor the fulfilment of the preconditions, adjusting them as necessary in response to changes in financial markets or other changes beyond the control of the government of the recipient country, prequalification would not avoid difficulties in relations between the Fund and the member concerned.

Transforming the Fund into an international lender of last resort would involve a fundamental departure from the underlying premises of the Bretton Woods system, which provided for the use of capital controls to deal with instability. In discussion of such a facility its introduction is frequently linked to concomitant arrangements regarding rights and obligations with respect to international capital transactions, together with a basic commitment to capital-account liberalization. This departure from the Bretton Woods arrangements is particularly notable in the report of the Meltzer Commission, which virtually proposes, *inter alia*, the discontinuation of all other forms of IMF

---

[9]   The concept belongs to Gerald Corrigan, quoted in Rogoff (1999: 27).

lending, including those for current account financing. Such a drastic shift in the nature of IMF lending, from current account to capital account financing, would lead to a further segmentation of the Fund's membership, with consequences for its governance and universality. Indeed, as noted by a former United States Treasury Secretary, only a small number of relatively prosperous emerging economies would be eligible for lender-of-last-resort financing.[10]

Moreover, under these proposals, a large majority of developing countries would be excluded from multilateral financing. The Meltzer Commission argued, throughout its discussion of lending policies by both the IMF and the World Bank, that current account financing to developing countries should, in principle, be provided by private markets. However, markets cannot always be relied on to fulfil this task properly. One of the original objectives of the IMF was to provide short-term financing when reserves were inadequate to meet current account needs resulting from temporary trading shocks and disturbances, while the World Bank was to meet longer-term financing needs of reconstruction and development. For temporary payments disequilibria, it was agreed that short-term financing was necessary in order to avoid sharp cuts in domestic absorption or disruptive exchange rate adjustments. Even when the effects of such shocks were deemed to be more lasting, IMF financing was believed to be necessary to allow orderly adjustment. Experience shows that financial markets often fail to meet such needs since they tend to be pro-cyclical, with the result that credit lines are cut off just when they are most needed. Given the increased instability of the external trading and financial environment of developing countries, a reform of the Bretton Woods institutions should seek to improve, rather than eliminate, counter-cyclical and emergency financing of the current account.

F.   GOVERNANCE OF INTERNATIONAL FINANCE

There are certainly conceptual and technical difficulties in designing effective global mechanisms for the prevention and manage-

---

[10] L.H. Summers, Testimony before the Banking Committee of the House of Representatives, 23 March 2000: 14.

ment of financial instability and crises. Such difficulties are also encountered in designing national financial safety nets, and explain why a fail-safe system is unreachable. At the international level there is the additional problem that any system of control and intervention would need to be reconciled with national sovereignty and accommodate the diversity among nations. Political constraints and conflicts of interest, including among the G-7 members themselves, rather than conceptual and technical problems, appear to be the main reason why the international community has not been able to achieve significant progress in setting up effective global arrangements.

So far the major industrial countries have not addressed the establishment of a multilateral system for international finance based on a few core principles and rules, preferring instead a strengthening of the financial systems of debtor countries in crisis prevention, and favouring a differentiated, case-by-case approach to crisis intervention. This approach not only has created asymmetry between debtors and creditors, but also has left far too much discretion with the major creditor countries, on account of their leverage in international financial institutions. It has kept out of the reform agenda many issues of immediate concern to developing countries, which are discussed in the following chapters. However, even a rules-based system raises concerns for developing countries: under the current distribution of power and governance of global institutions, such a system would be likely to reflect the interests of larger and richer countries rather than to redress the imbalances between international debtors and creditors. Such biases against developing countries already exist in the rules-based trading system, although relations here are more symmetrical than in the financial domain.

If reforms to the existing financial structures are to be credible, they must provide for greater collective influence from developing countries and embody a genuine spirit of cooperation among all countries, facing many different problems but sharing a common desire to see a more stable international financial and monetary system. No less than a fundamental reform of the governance of multilateral institutions is therefore necessary.[11] The areas in which

---

[11]   For an illuminating discussion of global governance issues, see Helleiner (2000).

reform is needed are explored in a study undertaken for the Group of 24 (G-24, the developing-country group at the IMF/World Bank institutions), which argues that governance within the Bretton Woods institutions needs to be improved regarding matters such as representation and ownership, accountability and transparency, and adaptation and change:

> The allocation of quotas and the correlate membership rights in both institutions no longer reflect the application of a coherent, justifiable set of principles: quotas no longer reflect relative economic and political power, and the principle of equal representation, which was once implemented by the allocation of "basic votes", has been significantly eroded. Furthermore, decision-making practices have not adapted to the changed mandates of both institutions, whose work now takes them further and further into influencing domestic policy choices in developing countries. (Woods, 1998: 95)

While, as recognized in that study, efforts have been made to respond to calls for more transparent, accountable and participatory governance, the basic modalities and procedures for taking decisions remain largely unchanged. Thus, whereas developed countries account for only 17 per cent of voting strength in the United Nations, 24 per cent in the WTO and 34 per cent in the International Fund for Agricultural Development (IFAD), they account for over 61 per cent in the Bretton Woods institutions. And a single country holds virtual veto power over important decisions such as capital increases or SDR allocations. It is now agreed in many quarters that the procedures for selection of the Managing Director of the IMF and the President of the World Bank should give greater weight to the views of developing and transition economies, since the *raison d'être* of these institutions is now to be found mainly in their mandates and operations with respect to these economies. More fundamentally, crucial decisions on global issues are often taken outside the appropriate multilateral forums in various groupings of major industrial countries such as the G-7 or G-10, where there is no developing-country representation or participation. Consequently, "nothing consequential happens in the formally constituted organizations that *do* have operational capabilities – the

IMF, the World Bank, the Bank for International Settlements – without the prior consent, and usually the active endorsement, of the 'Gs' (here used as a short form for all the deliberative groups and committees dominated by the major industrial countries)" (Culpeper, 2000: 5). The inclusion of developing countries in the discussions of financial architecture reform that take place outside the Bretton Woods institutions, notably in the newly created G-20, is thus generally welcomed as an important step in ensuring better participation and governance in international finance. However, even though its first chairman, the Canadian Finance Minister Paul Martin, declared that the G-20 "has a mandate to explore virtually every area of international finance and the potential to deal with some of the most visible and troubling aspects of today's integrated world economy",[12] so far the focus of its work has not substantially deviated from the G-7 reform agenda, including a stock-taking of progress made by all members in reducing vulnerabilities to crises, an evaluation of countries' compliance with international codes and standards, the completion of the so-called transparency reports, and an examination of different exchange rate regimes and their role in debtor countries in cushioning the impact of international financial crises (Culpeper, 2000: 19). Furthermore, despite the G-20's broader membership, there are still serious limitations on participation and accountability:

> The G-20 is severely flawed in that it contains no representation … from the poorest and smallest developing countries. … Presumably, this is because the poorest and smallest are unlikely ever to constitute any systemic threat. But there are major "architectural" issues surrounding the provision of adequate development finance to these countries and their peoples. … Nor does the G-20 possess any mechanisms either for reporting or for accountability to the broader international community, such as the constituency system provides within the IMF and World Bank, or any provisions for non-governmental inputs or transparency. (Helleiner, 2000: 13-14)

---

[12]   Paul Martin, Speech to the House of Commons Standing Committee on Foreign Affairs and International Trade, Ottawa, 18 May 2000.

A number of proposals have been made on how to reform the multilateral process as well as to improve the membership, accountability and reform agenda of the G-20. Certainly, progress in these areas will depend on the willingness of the major industrial countries to extend the reform agenda and process so that they also address the concerns of developing countries. It will depend no less on positions taken by developing countries themselves. As noted above, there is no consensus among the developing countries on several issues of the reform agenda. Many of the differences pertain to the modalities of official intervention in the management and resolution of financial crises. Most countries appear to give priority to access to large amounts of contingency financing as a defence against contagion and instability, despite their concerns as to the appropriateness of several of its features. At times of crisis many countries seem unwilling to impose temporary standstills, preferring official bailouts, even though they often complain that their terms and conditions deepen the crisis, put an unfair share of the burden of adjustment on the debtors, and allow the creditors to get away scot-free. This unwillingness may partly reflect an assessment that the risks of imposing a standstill are excessively high when such action is still considered an aberrant response to a crisis (so far resorted to by only a few countries).

There appears to be greater convergence of views and interests regarding measures for crisis prevention and governance of international finance. Objectives commonly shared by developing countries include: more balanced and symmetrical treatment of debtors and creditors regarding codes, transparency and regulation; more stable exchange rates among the major reserve currencies; effective IMF surveillance of the policies of the major industrial countries, especially with respect to their effects on capital flows, exchange rates and trade flows of developing countries; a less intrusive conditionality; and, above all, more democratic and participatory multilateral institutions and processes. Effective reform of the international monetary and financial system will ultimately depend on the ability and willingness of developing countries to combine their efforts around these common objectives, and on acceptance by developed countries that accommodating these objectives is essential to building a more inclusive system of global economic governance.

REFERENCES

Akyüz Y (2000). The debate on the international financial architecture: Reforming the reformers. UNCTAD Discussion Paper, 148. Geneva, April.

Akyüz Y and Cornford A (1999). Capital flows to developing countries and the reform of the international financial system. UNCTAD Discussion Paper, 143. Geneva, November.

Culpeper R (2000). Systemic reform at a standstill: A flock of "Gs" in search of global financial stability. Paper prepared for the Commonwealth Secretariat/World Bank Conference on Developing Countries and Global Financial Architecture, Marlborough House, London, 22-23 June.

Dam KW (1982). *The Rules of the Game. Reform and Evolution in the International Monetary System.* Chicago, University of Chicago Press.

Eatwell J and Taylor L (1998). International capital markets and the future of economic policy. CEPA Working Paper, 9. New York, Centre for Economic Policy Analysis, September.

Eatwell J and Taylor L (2000). *Global Finance at Risk: The Case for International Regulation.* New York, The New Press.

Edwards RW (1985). *International Monetary Collaboration.* Dobbs Ferry, NY, Transnational Publishers.

Eichengreen B and Portes R (2000). A shortsighted vision for IMF reform. *Financial Times,* 9 March.

Feldstein M (1998). Refocusing the IMF. *Foreign Affairs,* 77(2), March/April.

Fischer S (1999). On the need for an international lender of last resort. *The Journal of Economic Perspectives,* 13(4), fall.

Goldstein M (2000). Strengthening the international financial architecture. Where do we stand? Working Paper, 00-8. Washington, DC, Institute for International Economics, October.

Helleiner G (2000). Markets, politics and globalization: Can the global economy be civilized? 10th Raúl Prebisch Lecture. Geneva, UNCTAD, December.

IMF (2000). *Report of the Acting Managing Director to the International Monetary and Financial Committee on Progress in Reforming the IMF and Strengthening the Architecture of the International Financial System.* Washington, DC, International Monetary Fund, April.

Kaufman H (1992). Ten reasons to reform. *Euromoney,* November.

Raffer K (1990). Applying chapter 9 insolvency to international debts: An economically efficient solution with a human face. *World Development,* 18(2).

Rodrik D (1999). Governing the global economy: Does one architectural style fit all? Paper prepared for the Brookings Institution Trade Policy Forum Conference on Governing in a Global Economy, Harvard University,

April.

Rogoff K (1999). International institutions for reducing global financial instability. *The Journal of Economic Perspectives,* 13(4), fall.

Soros G (1998). Avoiding a breakdown. *Financial Times,* 31 December 1997 and 1 January 1998; and *The Crisis of Global Capitalism.* New York, Public Affairs Press.

Summers LH (2000). The troubling aspects of IMF reform. *Financial Times,* 23 March.

TDR (1986). *Trade and Development Report 1986.* United Nations publication, sales no. E.86.II.D.5. New York, United Nations Conference on Trade and Development.

TDR (1998). *Trade and Development Report 1998.* United Nations publication, sales no. E.98.II.D.6. New York and Geneva, United Nations Conference on Trade and Development.

TDR (2001). *Trade and Development Report 2001.* United Nations publication, sales no. E.01.II.D.10. New York and Geneva, United Nations Conference on Trade and Development.

Triffin R (1976). Jamaica: "major revision" or fiasco. In: Bernstein EM et al. *Essays in International Finance,* 115. Princeton, Princeton University, April.

UNCTAD secretariat (1987). The exchange rate system. In: UNCTAD, *International Monetary and Financial Issues for the Developing Countries.* United Nations publication, sales no. E.87.IID3. New York.

Williamson J (1983). *The Exchange Rate System.* Washington, DC, Institute for International Economics.

Wolf M (2000). Between revolution and reform – The Meltzer Commission's vision. *Financial Times,* 8 March.

Woods N (1998). Governance in international organizations: The case for reform in the Bretton Woods institutions. In: UNCTAD, *International Monetary and Financial Issues for the 1990s.* Vol. IX. United Nations publication, sales no. E.98.II.D.3. New York and Geneva.

Chapter 2

Standards and Regulation

Andrew Cornford

A. INTRODUCTION

MANY recent initiatives for international financial reform are directed at reaching agreement on, and implementation of, standards for major areas of economic policy. Most of these standards are ultimately intended to contribute to economic stability at both the national and international level. Their main proximate targets are the strengthening of domestic financial systems and the promotion of international financial stability "by facilitating better-informed lending and investment decisions, improving market integrity, and reducing the risks of financial distress and contagion" (FSF, 2000a, para. 23). In pursuit of these objectives, the standards cover not only the financial sector, but also aspects of macroeconomic policy and policy on disclosure. Many features of these standards reflect concerns arising out of the experience of recent financial crises, though in a number of cases they also build on initiatives involving mainly industrial countries and originating from events of the more distant past. While the standards themselves are designed to promote stability, their development can also be viewed as part of a process of arriving at a set of globally accepted rules for policy in the financial and monetary spheres. Such rules could furnish one of the prerequisites for the provision of international financial support for countries experiencing currency crises. In this sense, they are an international analogue of the national rules for the financial sector, compliance with which is a condition for lender-of-last-resort financing.

The Financial Stability Forum (FSF)[1] has identified a number of standards which it considers particularly relevant to strengthening financial systems. These vary in the precise degree to which they have received international endorsement, but they have been broadly accepted, in principle, as representing basic requirements for good practice. As can be seen from table 1, the standards cover the areas of macroeconomic policy and data transparency, institutional and market infrastructure, and financial regulation and supervision – areas that are closely interrelated in many ways. Macroeconomic policy, for example, can crucially affect the more sectoral dimensions of financial stability through its impact on the values of financial firms' assets and liabilities (and thus on the context in which financial regulation and supervision are conducted). It can also affect the functioning of the system for payments and settlement, which is at the heart of the infrastructure of financial markets. Similarly, effective financial regulation and supervision are inextricably related to accounting, auditing and insolvency procedures. Insurance products are frequently incorporated in, or sold in close conjunction with, investment products, thus increasing the channels through which disturbances affecting the market for one financial service can be transmitted to markets for another. And even such an apparently self-contained issue as money laundering has, on occasion, threatened the stability of financial firms.[2]

---

[1] The Financial Stability Forum was established by the finance ministers and central bank governors of the G-7 in February 1999 to promote international financial stability through improved exchange of information and cooperation with respect to financial supervision and surveillance. Its membership consists of the national authorities responsible for financial stability in selected OECD countries, Hong Kong (China) and Singapore, and major international financial institutions, international supervisory and regulatory bodies and central-bank expert groupings.

[2] An example of such dangers was furnished by the large-scale withdrawal of funds from and subsequent bankruptcy of two subsidiaries of Deak and Co. (Deak Perera Wall Street and Deak Perera International Banking Corporation) in response to information in a 1984 report of the United States Presidential Commission on Organized Crime concerning Deak Perera's involvement in money laundering.

The list of organizations associated with the key standards in table 1 is not exhaustive, and the standards themselves give only a brief idea of the many initiatives taking place under each heading. When the FSF reviewed the standards agenda in March 2000, the 12 subject areas were already only a subset of a larger group which eventually numbered 64 (FSF, 2000a, paras. 55-57 and Annex 8). The discussion in section B below focuses on the main thrust and contents of the standards in table 1. It also aims to illustrate some omissions and some of the practical problems posed by implementation of the standards. Section C looks at the process of participation in the formulation and application of the standards initiatives. This leads naturally to the issue of bias in the official thinking which underlies the selection of the subjects covered by these initiatives and the asymmetrical way in which they are approached. To illustrate the strengths and weaknesses of this thinking, three major reports of FSF working groups are examined in some detail. Section D deals more systematically with implementation issues and some of the problems already raised in the context of particular standards in section B. Various incentives and sanctions are discussed as well as the findings of a preliminary survey to review actual progress so far. As discussed in section E, the contribution of standards to the achievement of greater financial stability depends to a great extent on their incorporation into the rules and norms of business practice. This in turn is closely connected to the regulatory and supervisory regime within which these rules and norms are applied. However, improvements on this front have inherent limits, as illustrated by examples taken from the key area of banking super-vision.

B. THEMES OF THE KEY STANDARDS

Each of the codes discussed here is intended to accomplish improve-ments at both macroeconomic and microeconomic levels. A signifi-cant part of the impetus behind the initiatives discussed in subsections B.1-B.3 was furnished by particular financial crises and systemic incidents of stress – mostly recent ones. Their major objectives are macroeconomic or systemic, though particular features of the behav-iour of specific economic agents are also targeted. In the case of the

Table 1

KEY STANDARDS FOR FINANCIAL SYSTEMS

Subject Area	Key Standard	Issuing Body
Macroeconomic Policy and Data Transparency		
Monetary and financial policy transparency	Code of Good Practices on Transparency in Monetary and Financial Policies	IMF
Fiscal policy transparency	Code of Good Practices on Fiscal Transparency	IMF
Data dissemination	Special Data Dissemination Standard (SDDS) General Data Dissemination System (GDDS)[1]	IMF
Institutional and Market Infrastructure		
Insolvency	Principles and Guidelines on Effective Insolvency Systems[2]	World Bank
Corporate governance	Principles of Corporate Governance	OECD
Accounting	International Accounting Standards (IAS)[3]	IASC[4]
Auditing	International Standards on Auditing (ISA)	IFAC[4]
Payment and settlement	Core Principles for Systemically Important Payment Systems	CPSS
Market integrity	The Forty Recommendations of the Financial Action Task Force on Money Laundering	FATF
Financial Regulation and Supervision		
Banking supervision	Core Principles for Effective Banking Supervision	BCBS
Securities regulation	Objectives and Principles of Securities Regulation	IOSCO
Insurance supervision	Insurance Supervisory Principles	IAIS

Source: FSF (2000a: 19).

¹ Economies that have, or might seek, access to international capital markets are encouraged to subscribe to the more stringent SDDS and all other economies are encouraged to adopt the GDDS.
² The World Bank is co-ordinating a broad-based effort to develop these principles and guidelines. The United Nations Commission on International Trade Law (UNCITRAL), which adopted the *Model Law on Cross-Border Insolvency* in 1997, will help facilitate implementation.
³ The BCBS has reviewed relevant IAS, and a joint BCBS-IASC group is further considering bank-related issues in specific IAS. IOSCO has reviewed and recommended use of 30 IAS in cross-border listings and offerings, supplemented where necessary to address issues at a national or regional level. The IAIS's review of relevant IAS is ongoing.
⁴ The International Accounting Standards Committee (IASC) and the International Federation of Accountants (IFAC) are distinct from other standard-setting bodies in that they are private sector bodies.

codes discussed in subsections B.4-B.9, the balance between macroeconomic and microeconomic objectives is different, with much less explicit emphasis given to the former. Moreover, many of the latter codes are of long-standing origin and antedate the crises of the 1990s. It is their incorporation into a global programme of financial reform that is recent.

1.   Macroeconomic policy and data transparency

The Code of Good Practices on Transparency in Monetary and Financial Policies (IMF, 2000a) identifies desirable transparency practices in the conduct of monetary policy and of policies towards the financial sector. These practices require: clarity with respect to the roles, responsibilities and objectives of central banks and financial agencies other than central banks with responsibility for overseeing and supervising different parts of the financial sector; open processes for the formulation and reporting of decisions on monetary and financial policy; public availability of information concerning policies in both spheres; and accountability and assurances of integrity for the central bank, other financial agencies and their staff.

The Code of Good Practices on Fiscal Transparency (IMF, 1998) is based on four principles: first, the roles and responsibilities of and within the government should be transparent, and for this purpose there should be a clear legal and administrative framework for fiscal management; secondly, governments should commit themselves to public disclosure of comprehensive, reliable information on fiscal activities; thirdly, the process of budget preparation, execution and reporting should be open; and, fourthly, fiscal information should be subject to public and independent scrutiny.

The Special Data Dissemination Standard (SDDS, at: http://dsbb.imf.org/sddsindex.htm) was developed by the IMF in response to recognition, after the Mexican crisis, of widespread deficiencies in major categories of economic data available. It prescribes the data which countries intending to use the world's capital markets should be expected to make public concerning the real, fiscal, financial and external sectors of the economy, and it lays down minimum benchmarks to be met in terms of periodicity and timeliness in the provision of that information. Since its inception, the SDDS has been strengthened by the inclusion of a requirement to disclose not only reserve assets, but also reserve-related liabilities and other potential drains on reserves, such as short derivative positions and guarantees extended by the government for borrowing by the private sector in foreign currency. The SDDS is supplemented by the General Data Dissemination System (GDDS, at: http://dsbb.imf.org/gddsindex.htm), which is designed to improve the quality of data disclosed by all member countries of the IMF.

The rationale for these codes and standards has several facets. The effectiveness of monetary, financial and fiscal policies can be enhanced if the objectives and instruments of policy in these areas are known to the public and if the government's commitment to these objectives is credible. Good governance more generally requires that central banks, other financial agencies and fiscal authorities are accountable. But an important aspect of the Codes' rationale goes beyond their benefits at the domestic level and concerns international lenders and investors. Here, the idea is that transparency should help lenders and investors to evaluate and price risk more accurately, thus contributing to policy discipline in recipient countries. Moreover, the assessment of individual countries made possible by these Codes is expected to prevent the so-called contagion effect, whereby a loss of confidence in one country spreads to others simply because they belong to the same category or region.[3]

That transparency regarding major areas of macroeconomic policy can contribute to their credibility, and to good governance more generally, seems incontrovertible. Transparency is also capable of facilitating multilateral surveillance by organizations such as the IMF. Understandably, the Codes confine themselves to process rather than substance, since codes of rules for policy would be enormously complex if they were to cover the great variety of different situations and countries. In addition, it would be much more difficult to reach consensus on such rules than on those limited to process.

Regarding the expectation that either the Codes concerning macroeconomic policy or the SDDS will lead to much-improved decisions by international lenders and investors, and thus to improved resource allocation and enhanced policy discipline for the governments of the receiving countries, there are grounds for scepticism. The new disclosure rules of the SDDS failed to serve as an effective early warning system in the case of the Asian crisis. Indeed, information was widely available concerning the balance of payments of the countries involved, the external financial flows to them, their corporate governance, trends in their domestic lending and in their banks' exposure to overvalued property sectors, and major features of external assets and liabilities (though there were gaps in what was publicly disclosed concerning the last of these items, gaps which subsequent strengthening of the SDDS was designed to fill). And if the availability of pertinent data failed to deter capital flows associated with the build-up of eventually unsustainable external financial positions in certain Asian countries, the same applied, *a fortiori*, to the behaviour of international lenders and investors in the Russian Federation prior to the crisis of mid-1998.

A more fundamental limitation of the potential contribution of transparency to the prevention of financial instability is due to the considerable variation in accompanying macroeconomic conditions and other features of policy regimes – a variation evident during recent financial crises. A common characteristic of the countries affected by

---

[3] This part of the rationale for standards is particularly emphasized in Drage, Mann and Michael (1998: 77-78).

these crises was their openness to capital flows, but there were also substantial differences in many of their macroeconomic indicators and other features of their economies. These differences involved external deficits, the extent of currency overvaluations, the size of budget deficits, the relative importance of consumption and investment in the booms preceding the crises, the relative size of countries' external debt owed by the public and private sectors, and the coverage and effectiveness of regimes of financial regulation and supervision.

Analysis of recent international financial crises also points to other difficulties as to the extent to which improved disclosure of macroeconomic variables can contribute to greater financial stability, in particular to the avoidance of the contagion effect. National balance sheets do not always reflect the pressures on external payments that can result from the adjustment of derivative positions which are off-balance-sheet and not always adequately covered by accounting rules. Moreover, derivative positions, even if covered under these rules, are capable of blurring distinctions between different categories of exposure, such as those between short- and longer-term. There is now a consensus that cross-border hedging and other practices make many of the international financial system's fault lines difficult to identify in advance. As a recent report of the FSF states:

> Certain commonly employed risk management techniques ... can have the effect of adding to the volatility of both prices and flows in the international capital market ... That is, investors acquire or dispose of claims whose risk characteristics and price history resemble those of the asset being proxied but where the market is deeper, more liquid, or subject to fewer restrictions and controls. Such behaviour was one of the factors behind the large fluctuations in capital flows to South Africa and several countries in Eastern Europe around the time of the Asian crisis. (FSF, 2000b, para. 28)

In the context of more recent events, attention has been drawn to the way in which Brazilian bonds have become an instrument widely used by investors in emerging markets to hedge positions in the debt of other countries such as the Russian Federation, Morocco and the Republic of Korea.

2.   Banking supervision

Weaknesses in the banking sector and inadequate banking supervision[4] have played a central role in recent financial crises in developed as well as developing countries. Recognition of the increasing potential for destabilizing cross-border effects of banking crises – owing to the internationalization of the banking business – has led to initiatives since the 1970s that aim to improve international cooperation in banking regulation and supervision. Initially, these initiatives were directed primarily at banks in industrial countries and offshore financial centres in response to a number of events that highlighted the inadequacies in their banking regulation and supervision. These events provided much of the inspiration for subsequent efforts to improve regulatory and supervisory cooperation. The standards which emerged from these initiatives eventually also achieved widespread acceptance among developing and transition economies. The Basel Committee on Banking Supervision (BCBS) – the most important vehicle for most of these initiatives – has increasingly assumed the role of global standard-setter in this area.[5]

A major outcome of the BCBS's extension of the focus of its activities beyond the concerns of its member countries is the *Core Principles for Effective Banking Supervision* issued in late 1997. In the development of these Principles, the BCBS collaborated with supervisors of economies outside the G-10 (including several developing and transition economies). They cover seven major subject areas: (i)

---

[4] The distinction between banking regulation and supervision in the literature is not particularly clearcut. But regulation can be taken roughly to refer to rules, both those set out in banking legislation and those referring to the instruments and procedures of the competent authorities. Supervision refers to implementation including licensing, ongoing offsite and onsite supervision of institutions, enforcement and sanctioning, crisis management, the operation of deposit insurance, and procedures for handling bank insolvencies. These distinctions follow closely those in Lastra (1996: 108).

[5] The BCBS comprises representatives of the central banks and supervisory authorities of Belgium, Canada, France, Germany, Italy, Japan, Luxembourg, Netherlands, Sweden, Switzerland, United Kingdom and United States. For an account of the acceptance of the BCBS's standards beyond its membership, primarily in relation to prudential standards for bank capital, see Cornford (2000a, sect. III).

the preconditions for effective banking supervision; (ii) the licensing and structure of banks; (iii) prudential regulations and requirements; (iv) methods of ongoing supervision; (v) information requirements; (vi) the formal powers of supervisors; and (vii) cross-border banking. In April 1998, the BCBS undertook a survey of compliance with the Core Principles in 140 economies, an effort paralleled by IMF and World Bank reviews of compliance in selected countries.[6] Subsequently a Core Principles Liaison Group (CPLG) of 22 members[7] was set up to provide feedback to the BCBS on the practical implementation of these Principles. The reviews of compliance and feedback from the CPLG led to the development by the BCBS of the *Core Principles Methodology* issued in October 1999 (BCBS, 1999a).

This document on methodology is intended to provide guidance in the form of "essential" and "additional" criteria for the assessment of compliance by the different parties to which this task may be entrusted, such as the IMF, the World Bank, regional supervisory groups, regional development banks and consulting firms, but not the BCBS itself. In addition to the specific criteria relating to banking supervision, the assessors are also required to form a view as to the presence of certain more general preconditions regarding such subjects as: (i) sound, sustainable macroeconomic policies; (ii) a well-developed public infrastructure, including an adequate body of law covering, for example, contracts, bankruptcy, collateral and loan recovery, as well as accounting standards approaching those of international best practices; (iii) market discipline based on financial transparency, effective corporate governance and the absence of government intervention in banks' commercial decisions except in accordance with disclosed policies and guidelines; (iv) adequate supervisory procedures for dealing with problems in banks; and (v) adequate mechanisms for systemic protection such as a lender-of-last-

---

[6] For a discussion of these assessments of compliance, see IMF (2000b).

[7] The members of the CPLG are from Argentina, Australia, Brazil, Chile, China, Czech Republic, Commission Bancaire de l'Union Monétaire Ouest Africain, France, Germany, Hong Kong (China), India, Italy, Japan, Mexico, Netherlands, Republic of Korea, Russian Federation, Saudi Arabia, Singapore, South Africa, United Kingdom and United States. In addition, the CPLG has representatives from the European Commission, the Financial Stability Institute, the IMF and the World Bank.

resort facility or deposit insurance (or both). The parts of the assessment directed more specifically at banking supervision comprise not only the procedures of supervision but also its subject matter (which, of course, includes the standards for prudential regulation and for banks' own internal controls and risk management covered in the BCBS's own documents over the years). With respect to subjects such as accounting and auditing standards and insolvency law, the *Core Principles for Effective Banking Supervision* clearly overlap to some degree other key standards mentioned in table 1.

Assessment of compliance with the Core Principles requires evaluation of several related requirements, including prudential regulation and other aspects of the legal framework, supervisory guidelines, onsite examinations and offsite analysis, supervisory reporting and other aspects of public disclosure, and enforcement or its absence. Assessment is also required of the supervisory authority's skills, resources and commitment, and of its actual implementation of the Core Principles. If evaluation of the preconditions for effective supervision (mentioned earlier) and assessment of the criteria relating to supervision itself are considered together, the exercise covers substantial parts of a country's commercial law, its accounting and auditing standards, and to some extent the quality of its government's macroeconomic management.

The assessment of relevant laws, regulations and supervisory procedures would appear to be fairly straightforward, but that of supervisory capacity and the effectiveness of implementation more complex.[8] Thus, perhaps understandably, the annex to the *Core Principles Methodology*, which sets out the structure and methodology for assessment reports prepared by the IMF and the World Bank, focuses principally on the former set of subjects and not the latter.

---

[8] This is recognized in the IMF paper cited above concerning the experience of the early assessment exercises as follows: "Due to lack of manpower and time, the assessments are not always as in-depth as warranted to identify all the underlying weaknesses. It is also difficult to obtain a thorough understanding of the adequacy of supervisory staff numbers and skills, as well as the skills of commercial bankers. A genuine assessment of bank supervision requires in-depth onsite review – including interviews with supervisors and bankers – resulting in well-researched judgements on institutional capacity and supervisors' concrete achievements" (IMF, 2000b, para. 57).

Assessment of supervisory capacity and the effectiveness of implementation is generally likely to be feasible only through extended in-depth scrutiny. This would require a lengthy presence of the assessor in the country undergoing assessment, either in the form of a permanent presence, or through a process involving several visits. If the latter option were selected for the purpose (and it seems rather more likely to be acceptable and more in accord with normal procedures for IMF surveillance), an authoritative assessment of compliance with the Core Principles may take years.

Assessment of the more general preconditions for effective supervision is not mentioned in the annex to the *Core Principles Methodology*, but here, too, a lengthy exercise is likely to be necessary. In particular, assessment of the many dimensions of a country's legal regime and of its accounting and auditing standards requires evaluation not only of laws, regulations and principles promulgated by professional bodies (such as those of accountants), but also of their implementation, and of the way in which they are incorporated into rules and norms in practice.[9] Many features of countries' legal regimes and business norms reflect differences in historical roots and in compromises among social groups. Internationally promulgated standards can help upgrade national rules and norms, but many aspects of the process will be gradual, and the objective should not be uniform rules for all countries.[10]

At the level of the countries being assessed, such exercises will

---

[9] In 1996, for example, before the outbreak of the East Asian financial crisis, the ratio of capital to risk-weighted assets in the Republic of Korea, according to official estimates, was above 9 per cent. However, if accounting rules closer to international norms had been used, non-performing loans for the sector as a whole would have exceeded its combined capital funds (Delhaise, 1998: 115). By the mid-1990s, in a number of countries affected by the crisis, the capital standards of the 1988 Basel Accord were part of the legal regime for banks (*TDR 1998*, Part One, chap. III, box 3). But in the absence of proper rules for the valuation of banks' assets, this standard had little meaning for many of the institutions to which it was supposed to apply.

[10] For a survey of banks' accounting practices and other financial reporting under regulatory regimes in 23 mainly industrial countries that highlights the prevalence and extent of shortfalls from international best practice in the first half of the 1990s, see Cornford (1999, sect. III).

often place an additional burden on a limited supply of supervisory capacity. In time, this capacity can be expanded, but the training of a bank supervisor typically requires a considerable period. And once trained, a supervisor may be faced with attractive alternative employment opportunities in the private sector, or even in the IMF or the World Bank themselves (which have recently been increasing the number of their staff with expertise in this area). There is, of course, awareness of the problem of human resources among bodies such as the BCBS, the IMF, the World Bank and the CPLG, and efforts are being made to coordinate initiatives and to ensure that scarce expert resources are used in the most efficient way. However, there remains a real danger that international assessment of countries' supervision will be at the expense of actual supervision on the ground.

3.   Payments and settlement

Payment systems enable the transfer of funds between financial institutions on their own behalf and on behalf of their customers, a role which makes such systems a potential source of systemic risk. This role is evident from a consideration of four key dimensions of an economy's flow-of-funds process: (i) the activities of various economic agents; (ii) the markets for financial instruments, assets and liabilities; (iii) the supporting infrastructure, of which an integral component is the payments system; and (iv) economic conditions binding the markets together and ensuring that they clear. Failures in any of the first three dimensions are capable of disrupting links between the markets and between economic agents whose mutual interdependence is based on several different kinds of transaction and exposure. If large, such disruptions can easily take on a systemic character.[11] Moreover, payment systems also play an essential role in foreign exchange transactions, which are thus an interface between

---

[11] This framework for analyzing policies aimed at the stability of the financial sector is frequently deployed by William White of the BIS (White, 1996: 23).

different countries' payment systems.[12] As a result of the links and similarities between systems of payment and settlement for fund transfers and for transactions in other financial assets, the main vehicle for international initiatives in this area, the BIS Committee on Payment and Settlement Systems (CPSS), has extended its purview beyond fund transfers to settlement systems for securities and foreign exchange and to clearing arrangements for exchange-traded derivatives (White, 1998:196-198). Moreover, the specific stability issues posed by securities settlement are currently the subject of a joint working group of the CPSS and the International Organization of Securities Commissions (IOSCO).[13] But the discussion here will be limited to the key standard in the area of payment and settlement mentioned in table 1.

The initiative to develop an internationally agreed framework of core principles for the design, operation and oversight of payment and settlement systems reflects increased recognition of the risks associated with rapidly rising volumes of payments (CPSS, 2000a).[14] The main risks in these systems are: *credit risk*, when a counterparty is unable to meet obligations within the system currently or in future;

---

[12]   Traditionally, such transactions have depended on national payment systems for the transfer of funds between correspondent banks of the countries whose currencies are involved. For example, in the case of a cross-border payments order transmitted between banks through SWIFT (Society for Worldwide Interbank Financial Telecommunication – a private company which transmits financial messages for the benefit of its shareholding member banks and of other approved categories of financial institutions in 88 countries), the banks must arrange the clearing and settlement themselves, either relying on mutual bilateral correspondent relationships or forwarding the orders to domestic systems for interbank fund transfers. Many major banks have introduced "straight-through processing", in which there is an automated linkage between their SWIFT connection and their computers linked to the domestic payments system (BIS, 1997: 482-485). More recently there has been growth in the direct settlement of foreign exchange transactions between parties in different jurisdictions through systems processing payments in more than one currency.

[13]   IOSCO is a grouping of securities regulators (both governmental and self-regulatory bodies) from more than 90 countries. Created in 1984, it is a private, non-profit organization whose main objectives are cooperation for better market regulation, information exchange, standard setting, and mutual assistance in the interest of protecting market integrity.

[14]   For a commentary on the Core Principles and discussion of the initiative's background, see Sawyer and Trundle (2000). (John Trundle of the Bank of England was chairman of the Task Force which drew up the Core Principles.)

liquidity risk (clearly closely related, but not identical, to credit risk), when a counterparty has insufficient funds to meet obligations within the system, though it may be able to do so at some future time; *legal risk*, when an inadequate legal framework or legal uncertainties cause or exacerbate credit or liquidity risks; and *operational risk*, when factors such as technical malfunctions or operational mistakes cause or exacerbate credit or liquidity risks. As discussed above, any of these risks can have systemic consequences, as the inability of a counterparty or counterparties to meet obligations within the system can have a domino effect on the ability of other counterparties to meet their obligations, and thus, ultimately, threaten the stability of the financial sector as a whole.[15] The task force established to develop the Core Principles was to limit itself to "systemically important payment systems", namely those capable of triggering or transmitting shocks across domestic and international financial markets.

The first Core Principle is directed at legal risk and specifies the need for a robust legal basis for the payment system, a requirement that links its rules and procedures to related areas of law such as those concerning banking, contract and insolvency. The second and third Principles concern rules and procedures for enabling participants to have a clear understanding of the system's impact on financial risks. They also recognize the need for defining how credit and liquidity risks are to be managed and for identifying responsibilities for this purpose. A system's risks can be exacerbated by the length of time required for final settlement or by the nature of the asset used to settle claims. Thus the fourth and sixth Principles specify the need for prompt settlement and for a settlement asset that is either a claim on the central bank or one carrying little or no credit risk (owing to the negligible risk of its issuer's failure). The fifth Principle requires a minimum standard of

---

[15] More specifically, the initiative was a response to the conclusion in the report of an ad hoc working party on financial stability in emerging-market economies, set up after the 1996 summit of the G-7, concerning the essential role of sound payment systems in the smooth operation of market economies, as well as to growing concern regarding the subject among emerging-market economies themselves. See mimeograph document of the Working Party on Financial Stability in Emerging Market Economies, *Financial stability in emerging market economies: A strategy for the formulation, adoption and implementation of sound principles and practices to strengthen financial systems* (April 1997, chap. II).

robustness for multilateral netting systems.[16] The seventh Principle is intended to minimize operational risk through ensuring a high degree of security and operational reliability. The eighth, ninth and tenth Principles address the more general issues of the system's efficiency and practicality (including the need for explicit recognition of any trade-off between safety and efficiency). They also address the need for objective and publicly disclosed criteria for participation in the system, permitting fair and open access, and effective, accountable and transparent governance arrangements. The Core Principles attribute to central banks key responsibility for ensuring that payment systems comply with the Principles.

The second part of the Report on the *Core Principles for Systemically Important Payment Systems* provides details on issues such as the identification of systemically important payment systems, the modalities of their review and reform, structural, technical and institutional factors to be considered, and the kinds of cooperation necessary with participants in the system, user groups and other parties to the reform process (CPSS, 2000b).[17] The second part also takes up certain cross-border aspects of payment systems. The Core Principles are now included in the joint IMF-World Bank Financial Sector Assessment Programme (FSAP).[18] However, experience in industrial countries suggests that the upgrading of payment systems required by the Principles is likely to entail a lengthy process owing to the many different actions required and the many different parties involved.

4.   Accounting and auditing

Improvements in financial reporting and transparency are essential to most of the initiatives on codes and principles, but in the area of accounting and auditing in table 1 there is an explicit aim to harmonize

---

[16]   In a multilateral netting arrangement, a participant nets obligations *vis-a-vis* other participants as a group throughout a specified period (typically a day), and then settles the debit or credit balance outstanding at the end of this period through the arrangement's common agent.

[17]   Part 2 was a response to widespread comments elicited by Part 1 that more detail on interpretation and implementation was needed.

[18]   This Programme is aimed at assessing the vulnerabilities of countries' financial sectors and identifying priorities for action, partly in the light of internationally agreed standards for these sectors.

standards. Through their impact on disclosure, these standards have an obvious bearing on counterparties' ability to assess the financial risks of transactions. The need for international harmonization is also due to the growth in cross-border business, especially in lending and investment. The principal body with responsibility for promulgating international accounting standards is the International Accounting Standards Committee (IASC).[19] Much of the recent work of the IASC has been directed at reaching a compromise on a set of standards acceptable both to the United States and to other member countries, and which satisfies disclosure requirements for the issuance and trading of securities in the world's major financial markets. A number of the difficult problems here concern the reconciliation of the understandably pluralistic approach of the IASC with the more specific and constraining rules of the Generally Accepted Accounting Principles (GAAP) of the United States.[20]

While debate on the International Accounting Standards (IAS) is concerned mainly with highly specific subjects,[21] its impact on the international financial system is likely to depend more on its success in raising standards of accounting and financial reporting worldwide. And this will also be related to accompanying initiatives to raise auditing standards. The targets of such efforts include internal auditing (i.e., assessment of the extent and effectiveness of a firm's manage-

---

[19] The IASC was created in 1973 by major professional accounting bodies and now includes more than 130 such bodies from more than 100 countries. The entities concerned with international accounting standards include not only professional accounting bodies, international accounting firms, transnational corporations and other international lenders and investors, but also other bodies such as international trade unions concerned with cross-border business activities.

[20] A 1997 study of the United States Financial Accounting Standards Board (FASB) identified 255 variations between United States and international standards, many of which were judged as significant. See Scott and Wellons (2000: 67). For a more extended discussion of the IASC-US Comparison Project, which was the source of this finding, see Grossfeld (2000).

[21] Specific topics identified as the most difficult for the achievement of reconciliation and understanding among countries in a survey of institutional investors, firms, underwriters and regulators in the first half of the 1990s (quoted in Iqbal, Melcher and Elmallah, 1997: 34) were the following: accounting for goodwill, deferred taxes, inventory valuation, depreciation methods, discretionary reserves, fixed-asset valuation, pensions, foreign currency transactions, leases, financial statement consolidation and financial disclosure requirements.

ment and accounting controls and of the safeguarding and efficient use of its assets) as well as external auditing (i.e., auditing of financial statements and supporting evidence to determine the conformity of the former with applicable standards). Internal auditing is now a legal requirement in several countries, and auditing committees have frequently acquired greater importance in countries where shifts in corporate governance have resulted in increased power for boards of directors *vis-a-vis* senior operating executives. But it is external auditing which is the principal subject of international initiatives. Here the problems of harmonization relate partly to differences in the accounting standards underlying financial statements but also to divergences in audit standard-setting processes themselves. These divergences result, for example, from the fact that in some countries auditing standards are set by the accounting profession whereas in others they are based on requirements mandated in laws and regulations, or they result from a process involving the joint participation of both the accounting profession and the government. The institution specified in table 1 as having the lead responsibility for international harmonization of auditing standards is the International Federation of Accountants (IFAC),[22] which closely collaborates with other bodies also occupying key positions in this area such as IOSCO and relevant EU institutions.

While improved standards of accounting and auditing have the potential for contributing to better decision-making by lenders and investors through enhanced transparency, recent experience cautions against exaggerated expectations in this regard, especially in the short run. There is also a question as to how far the greater transparency – which is the main ultimate objective under this heading – leads to greater financial stability. As the celebrated investment manager, Warren Buffett, warns, "the accountants' job is to record, not to evaluate", and "... the business world is simply too complex for a single set of rules to effectively describe reality for all enterprises" (Cunningham, 2000: 196, 202). In the case of financial firms, the

---

[22] The IFAC was established in 1977 to promulgate international standards in auditing and closely related subjects. The IFAC and IASC have an agreement of "mutual commitments" for close cooperation and mutual consultations, and membership in one automatically entails membership in the other.

difficulties are multiplied by the speed with which assets and liabilities can change, even in cases where high standards of reporting are observed. Moreover, as already noted, although financial reporting was poor in several of the countries involved in recent financial crises, there was no shortage of information available to lenders and investors about key macroeconomic variables and the general economic and legal environment in the countries concerned. And if the information in good financial reporting has such a beneficial effect on decision-making, why were lenders and investors not more wary in its absence, especially in view of weaknesses which should have been evident from the macroeconomic information which was available?

5. Corporate governance

Corporate governance involves the relationships between the management of a business and its board of directors, its shareholders and lenders, and its other stakeholders such as employees, customers, suppliers and the community of which it is a part. The subject thus concerns the framework in which the business objectives are set and how the means of attaining them and otherwise monitoring performance are determined. The *OECD Principles of Corporate Governance* (OECD, 1999) cover five basic subjects: (i) protection of the rights of shareholders, a heading that includes allowing the market for corporate control to function efficiently, transparently and fairly for all shareholders; (ii) equitable treatment of shareholders, including minority and foreign shareholders, with full disclosure of material information and the prohibition of abusive self-dealing and insider trading; (iii) recognition and protection of the exercise of the rights of stakeholders as established by law, and encouragement of cooperation between corporations and stakeholders in creating wealth, jobs and financially sound enterprises; (iv) timely and accurate disclosure and transparency with respect to matters relevant to company performance, ownership and governance, which should include an annual audit conducted by an independent auditor; and (v) a framework of corporate governance to ensure strategic guidance for the company and effective monitoring of its management by the board of directors, as well as the board's accountability to the company and shareholders (certain key functions of the board being specified under this heading).

Corporate governance sets rules on matters where variations of approach among countries are often rooted in societal differences – for example, with respect to the relative importance of family-owned firms as opposed to corporations, or to prevalent norms regarding the primacy of sometimes conflicting business objectives, such as long-term sustainability, on the one hand, and value for shareholders, on the other. These societal differences, in turn, generally reflect differences in national histories and in the political and social consensus which has grown out of them.[23] The preamble to the OECD Principles acknowledges that there is no single model of good corporate governance and the Principles themselves are fairly general. They avoid rules for the more contentious aspects of relations between companies and their lenders and investors, such as appropriate levels of leverage. They also avoid the more detailed rules for the market for corporate control. Nevertheless, there remains a danger that the technical assistance and assessment exercises associated with the promulgation of these Principles – which will also involve other organizations such as the World Bank – will contain features that reflect biases in favour of concepts linked to particular models of corporate governance, most notably those of the United Kingdom or the United States.

Regarding the potential of better corporate governance to contribute to financial stability, a conclusion similar to that for auditing and accounting seems in order. Improvements in this area can be expected to lead to better decision-making on several matters, but if they are based on principles similar to those enunciated by the OECD, they are likely to be gradual. Moreover, the better decision-making achieved in this way may have only limited effects on instability, which results from forces which corporate governance can mitigate but not eliminate. These forces include the pressures on loan officers to achieve target levels of profit in financial firms (a chronic problem, but one still not satisfactorily addressed in most firms' internal controls), weakness in even state-of-the-art techniques for controlling credit, market and other financial risks, and psychological factors conducive to imitative and herd behaviour in the financial sector.

---

[23]   This point is forcefully made with the support of a wealth of case studies from the business history of the United States in Kennedy (2000, part 1).

6. Insolvency

Insolvency rules are such a substantial part of corporate governance as defined above that they have generated a separate literature on the subject. There is general recognition that existing regimes for insolvency are characterized by widespread weaknesses, or indeed by their total absence in some situations and countries.[24] At the national level (particularly in many developing and transition economies), weakness is associated with problems regarding the enforcement of contracts, ineffective modalities for the netting, clearance and settlement of outstanding obligations, poorly functioning arrangements for the collateral and security of loans, and conflicts of law. All these features can pose serious problems for certain aspects of the valuation of firms and securities, and they can be a source of increased financial risk. Their presence in emerging markets can therefore be a significant deterrent to foreign investment.

The lead role in developing globally acceptable rules for insolvency has been attributed to the World Bank, whose objective is to develop an "integrated matrix" of components and criteria for such rules, highlighting existing best practices.[25] These elements are intended to be a complement of a country's legal and commercial system with guidance provided as to how they would interact with and affect the system. Consensus on them is to be developed through a series of assessment exercises and international insolvency symposia. The principal focus of the World Bank's initiative is national regimes in developing and transition economies.

The feedback from this process has led to a Consultation Draft organized into the following three parts: (i) legal, institutional, regulatory, and restructuring and rehabilitation building blocks; (ii) different categories of insolvency conditions such as systemic insolvency and that of banks and enterprises; and (iii) an international dimension concerned with encouraging developing and transition economies to

---

[24] The arrangements proposed below, in Chapter 4, section B, for orderly workouts in the case of cross-border debt depend, for their functioning, on adequate national insolvency regimes.

[25] The account which follows relies heavily on the Group of Thirty (2000, chap. 2, sect. 1).

take account of both international best practices and issues with a cross-border dimension in order to facilitate their access to international financial markets.

Improved insolvency rules have a more direct link to financial stability than many of the other subjects covered by the codes in table 1. Their main role under this heading is to help contain the problems due to the insolvencies of particular firms and to prevent broader contagion effects. The beneficial impact of this role obviously extends to cross-border lending and investment. However, as noted above, the focus of the initiative being led by the World Bank is on rules for developing and transition economies, even though cross-border insolvencies (i.e., insolvencies involving firms with business entities in more than one country) pose difficult problems of coordination and conflicts of law in developed countries as well. Here the danger is that the insolvency of a large firm with an extensive international network of entities could seriously disrupt cross-border transactions. A special threat is that posed by the possibility of the failure of a large multinational bank having a home jurisdiction in a developed country.[26] Most of the problems which would result from such a failure concern the cross-border dimensions of insolvency, and attempts to develop international rules are currently concentrated in other forums.[27]

7.   Securities regulation

The *Objectives and Principles of Securities Regulation*, published by IOSCO in September 1998, sets out three major objectives:

---

[26] This point was made recently in an OECD publication: "The incidence of banking crises, and the costs these have imposed on countries, is quite large and the systemic consequences of the failure of a large institution are of a different order of magnitude from those associated with the failure of smaller institutions. In particular, the costs of bailing out a very big institution might be large relative to the resources of the country in which the institution resides. ... it is not clear that an increase in size and perhaps geographic scope of an institution makes the risk of its failure any greater than before. Accidents do happen, however, and it is likely that the systemic consequences of bank failures grow as institutions become larger and larger. The situation is also more complex in the case of internationally operating banks" (OECD, 2000a: 138-139).

[27] See Group of Thirty (2000, especially chaps. 4-6). The policy issues are surveyed in Group of Thirty (1998).

the protection of investors; ensuring that markets are fair, efficient and transparent; and the reduction of systemic risk. To achieve these objectives, it lists 30 principles covering responsibilities of the regulator, self-regulation, enforcement of securities regulation, cooperation in regulation domestically and internationally, the responsibilities of issuers, rules and standards for collective investment schemes, requirements for market intermediaries, and rules and standards for the secondary market. The principles explicitly related to systemic risk are covered mainly under the last two headings, and are concerned with capital and prudential standards for market intermediaries, procedures for dealing with the failure of a market intermediary, and systems for clearing and settling securities transactions which minimize such risk. In other words, the focus of the principles for reducing systemic risk is on measures directed at firms and market infrastructure.

Unsurprisingly for a code produced by a global organization of specialist regulators, these principles are concerned mainly with the fairness and efficient functioning of markets themselves. Connections to broader issues of macroeconomic policy and to policy towards the financial sector, both of which have been associated with systemic instability in developing and transition economies, are ignored. A more comprehensive and representative set of principles for securities markets – including issues highlighted by recent crises in developing and transition economies – should arguably address some aspects of policy towards the capital account of the balance of payments (such as appropriate conditions for the access of foreign portfolio investors) and the commercial presence of foreign investment institutions.

8.   Insurance

Traditionally, insurance is not regarded as a source of systemic risk. Consequently, the principal objectives of its regulation and supervision are client protection and the closely related subjects of the safety and soundness of insurance companies and their proper conduct of business. This involves such matters as disclosure, honesty, integrity and competence of firms and employees, marketing practices, and the objectivity of advice to customers. The principal grounds for downplaying the systemic risks of the insurance sector are that companies' liabilities are long-term and not prone to runs, while their assets are typically liquid. Moreover, mutual linkages among insurance companies and linkages between such companies and other financial firms are limited owing to the lack of a role for the former in clearing and payments and to the extent and depth of the markets where their assets are traded (Goodhart et al., 1998:14).

However, recently questions have been raised as to the adequacy of this characterization. This is partly due to the expanding role of the insurance sector in savings and investment products stemming from the close links between many kinds of life insurance policy and personal saving or investment instruments. The recent expansion is due partly to trends in the conglomeration of financial firms that have witnessed more widespread involvement of insurance companies in the sale and management of investment funds, on the one hand, and of banks in the insurance business, on the other. These trends have increased the possibility of contagion between insurance and other forms of financial business and, where large firms are involved, the scale of the possible adverse consequences of such contagion. In the case of developing and transition economies, an additional danger should be taken into account, namely, that the failure of one or more financial firms – including those with substantial insurance interests – may trigger a run on the currency. The resulting depreciation can have adverse consequences extending well beyond the sector where the problems originate.

The focus of the *Insurance Core Principles*[28] is the organization and practice of the sector's supervision, as well as the following sector-specific subjects: the corporate governance of insurance companies, their internal controls, prudential rules, conduct-of-business issues and the supervision of cross-border business. The prudential rules cover the management of an insurance company's assets, the identification and classification of liabilities, rules for capital requirements and for the use, disclosure and monitoring of derivatives and other off-balance-sheet items, and reinsurance as an instrument for risk containment. The principle covering the supervision of cross-border business

---

[28] For more detailed guidelines for the Principles' application, see International Association of Insurance Supervisors (IAIS, 2000b). The IAIS is an association of insurance supervisors established in 1994 and now includes supervisors from more than 100 countries.

operations is designed to ensure that no cross-border insurance entity escapes supervision, and that adequate arrangements are in place for consultations and information exchange between such an entity's home-country and host-country supervisors. Thus the focus of the *Insurance Core Principles* is functional, while issues explicitly relating to the supervision of financial conglomerates are left to other forums (IAIS, 2000a).[29]

9. Market integrity and money laundering

Money laundering is one of the most politically sensitive subjects covered by the codes and principles listed in table 1. It is an area where financial supervision interfaces directly with law enforcement – including some of the latter's tougher manifestations – since the activities financed with laundered money include drug dealing and terrorism. Indeed, the attention given to money laundering reflects, to a significant extent, the political difficulties in major developed countries in dealing with the problem of drug consumption. The policies adopted here have focused mainly on repression of production and consumption as opposed to alternative approaches, with the result that profits from illegal supply remain high. Money laundering is also closely connected to corrupt activities in developed and developing countries since it is used for concealing the size, sources and recipients of the money involved in such activities. Generally accepted estimates of the global scale of money laundering do not yet exist, but there is no doubt that it is very large. Money laundering has long been an important issue in relations between OECD countries and offshore financial centres. However, some recent scandals indicate that it also

---

[29] The main forum dealing explicitly with these issues is the Joint Forum on Financial Conglomerates, which was founded in 1996 and brings together developed-country representatives from the BCBS, IOSCO and IAIS. The Joint Forum has reviewed various means of facilitating the exchange of information among supervisors within their own sectors and among supervisors in different sectors, and has investigated legal and other barriers that impede the exchange of information among supervisors within their own sectors and between supervisors in different sectors. It has also examined other ways to enhance supervisory coordination, and is working on developing principles for the more effective supervision of regulated firms within financial conglomerates.

remains a problem for countries with traditional financial centres.[30] The principal international body entrusted with the task of combating money laundering is the Financial Action Task Force on Money Laundering (FATF),[31] established after the G-7 summit in 1989. Its current membership consists of 29 (mainly developed) countries and two international organizations – the European Commission and the Gulf Cooperation Council. In 1990, the FATF drew up a list of 40 recommendations which members are expected to adopt. These were revised in 1996 to take account of experience gained in the meantime and of changes in money laundering practices (FATF, 1999). Implementation by member countries of these recommendations is monitored on the basis of a two-pronged approach – an annual self-assessment exercise and periodic peer reviews of a member country by teams drawn from other members. More recently, the FATF has also conducted an exercise to identify jurisdictions deemed to be non-cooperative in the combat against money laundering (FATF, 2000). It clearly hopes that identification and the attendant publicity will prompt improvements in the 15 countries it has identified so far. In addition, its members have agreed to issue advisories to regulated financial institutions within their jurisdictions, requiring them to take extra care in business undertaken with counterparties in the 15 countries – an action that is likely to impose extra costs on such business.

The FATF's 40 recommendations include the following obligations: criminalization of the laundering of the proceeds of serious crimes; the identification of all customers and the keeping of appropri-

---

[30] See, for example, the coverage of recent events of money laundering in London in the *Financial Times*, 20 October 2000, and of a report of the subcommittee of the United States Senate concerning use of correspondent services provided by the country's banks for the purpose of money laundering in the *International Herald Tribune*, 6 February 2001. A *New York Times* editorial reproduced in the latter commented as follows: "Banks are undoubtedly wary of legal restrictions that raise costs and discourage depositors, particularly in their lucrative private banking divisions. But America cannot condemn corruption abroad while allowing its own banks to make fortunes off it."

[31] Various other regional or international bodies, either exclusively or as part of their work, also participate in combating money laundering. These include the Asia/Pacific Group on Money Laundering (APG), the Caribbean Financial Action Task Force (CFATF), the PC-R-EV Committee of the Council of Europe, and the Offshore Group of Banking Supervisors.

ate records; a requirement that financial institutions report suspicious transactions to the competent national authority and that they develop programmes to counter money laundering, including comprehensive internal controls and employee training; adequate supervision of money laundering and the sharing of expertise by supervisors with other domestic judicial and law enforcement authorities; and the strengthening of international cooperation through information exchange, mutual legal assistance and bilateral and multilateral agreements. There are relations between the FATF's initiatives and others directed at offshore financial centres.[32] For example, the harmful tax competition techniques for evading tax through recourse to offshore financial centres that are the subject of the OECD initiative (OECD, 2000b) are often the same as or similar to those used in money laundering. Likewise, "know your client" rules – a standard part of an effective regime for financial regulation – generally cover much the same ground as the FATF's requirements concerning customer identification. However, as in the case of other codes and principles discussed in this section, the contributions of the FATF's recommendations to international financial stability are mostly indirect.

Disclosures about involvement in money laundering have sometimes been associated with the failure of financial firms. However, money laundering – like the facilities offered by offshore financial centres – has played, at most, a marginal role in recent financial crises. Nevertheless, by making certain types of capital flight more difficult or costly, better control of money laundering can help restrain certain potentially destabilizing capital flows as well as the accumulation of external debt not linked to legitimate economic activity. But the effectiveness of such restraint will depend on the degree of active cooperation between countries which are sources and recipients of laundered money. Rules on money laundering are therefore an essential component of regulatory regimes for financial firms; without them such regimes could scarcely be characterized as effective or comprehensive.

---

[32] Attention is drawn to such connections between different international initiatives concerning offshore financial centres by José Roldan, President of the FATF during the period July 2000-2001, in an interview (Roldan, 2000: 21-22).

C.   INFLUENCE AND PARTICIPATION IN THE FORMULATION AND IMPLEMENTATION OF STANDARDS

Since standards became an integral component of international financial reform, much emphasis has been placed on the importance of "ownership" of their adoption and implementation by the countries affected. Extensive consultation has taken place as part of the assessment of implementation now under way and the results can eventually be expected to affect the future development of the standards themselves. However, not all of the exercises under this heading have been free of asymmetries among the different parties involved. This has led, on occasion, to questions about fairness. Lack of symmetry, particularly in the degree to which developing countries' concerns are taken into account, is also evident in the selection of subjects to which some of the standards are to apply. This would appear, at least partly, to reflect divergences in viewpoints concerning the functioning of the international financial system and the issues appropriate for policy action.

"Ownership" is related to countries' perceptions of their national interest in the adoption and implementation of standards. Such perceptions can be assisted by the exchange of experiences in forums such as the multilateral financial institutions and the standards-setting bodies, providing the opportunity to contribute to standards setting, alignment of programmes for standards implementation with domestic agendas for financial reform, and encouraging and aiding self-assessment (FSF, 2000a: 2). The promotion of country ownership is an objective of outreach programmes on standards implementation (IMF, 2000c), which operate through vehicles such as technical assistance, workshops and regional meetings. These activities have also involved the IMF and the World Bank, institutions with relevant expertise such as supervisors from major industrial countries, and others participating in processes of peer review.

The asymmetries mentioned above are not omnipresent and are not always easily identified, since they are often woven into basic assumptions or categories underlying the standards in table 1. The bias in some of the codes towards subjects likely to be of greater concern to developed countries often reflects the historical origins of the initiatives in question. Much of the cross-border business affecting the subjects covered was traditionally between parties in industrial countries, with developing countries' involvement being only fairly recent. Yet despite their increasing prominence in this context, certain concerns of developing countries appear to have been set aside during standards formulation and their interests ignored or downplayed during the follow-up. Moreover, parts of policy documents, the issuance of which has coincided with the standards initiatives – and which treat important parts of their rationale – in some cases substantially reflect official viewpoints in major developed countries, as evident from recent reports of the FSF.

For example, the report of the FSF's Working Group on Capital Flows (FSF, 2000b) focuses mainly on improved risk-management practices and enhanced transparency on the part of private and public sectors in countries receiving international lending and investment as the principal means of countering the instability of these flows.[33] The report also identifies various biases or incentives in the policies of recipient countries that are likely to lead to excessive dependence on short-term (and thus potentially volatile) inflows. But it downplays the impact of the behaviour of lenders and investors in developed countries as well as the effects of macroeconomic policies in these countries on capital flows to developing and transition economies. The report gives considerable attention to improvements in the provision and use of official statistics and of information in financial reporting by the private sector in recipient countries. However, it shies away from endorsing a requirement for frequent disclosure of data on the large short-term positions in assets denominated in a country's currency held by foreign firms other than banks (a category that includes hedge funds), which several developing (and some developed) countries perceive as threats to the stability of their exchange rates and financial markets.

Similarly, the report of the FSF Working Group on Highly Leveraged Institutions (HLIs)[34] has tended to play down widely

---

[33] For a more detailed commentary on this report, see Cornford (2000b).

[34] This FSF report focuses mainly on large, substantially unregulated institutions characterized by low transparency, primarily hedge funds. But, as the report notes, a clear distinction cannot always be drawn between the practices of these institutions and others subjected to greater regulation.

expressed concerns of certain countries in some of its policy recommendations (FSF, 2000c). This Working Group distinguished between two broad groups of issues posed by HLIs: systemic risks (of the kind exemplified by the collapse of Long Term Capital Management (LTCM)), on the one hand, and "market dynamics issues" (i.e., the amplification of instability and the threats to market integrity which may result from HLIs' operations in "small- and medium-sized open" economies), on the other. The systemic risks which may be caused by HLIs are naturally of concern to developing and transition economies. Like other participants in international financial markets, for example, they were affected by the increases in risk premiums and the sharply reduced availability of financing in late 1998, to which the collapse of LTCM contributed. Nevertheless, their special concerns are related more to the "market dynamics issues".

The Working Group conducted an examination of "market dynamics issues" in the experiences of six economies during 1998.[35] Its conclusions amounted to a qualified endorsement of concerns which had been expressed regarding HLIs. Thus the capacity of HLIs to establish large and concentrated positions in small- and medium-sized markets was acknowledged, and with this, their potential to exert a destabilizing influence. But there was less consensus as to the importance of their influence in comparison with other factors during particular instances of instability in the different economies during 1998. Similar conclusions were reached regarding the threat to market integrity posed by some aggressive practices attributed to HLIs, such as heavy selling of currencies in illiquid markets, dissemination of rumours about future developments, selective disclosure of information about firms' positions and strategies, and correlated position-taking in the markets for different assets within a country and also across currencies with the objective of achieving profitable move-

---

[35] The six economies were Australia, Hong Kong (China), Malaysia, New Zealand, Singapore and South Africa.

ments in relative prices.[36] Here, too, the capacity of HLIs to engage in such practices was recognized, but there was less agreement as to its significance at different times and in different countries.

The major thrust of the Working Group's recommendations is directed at reducing the systemic risk HLIs are capable of causing rather than at "market dynamics issues". The recommendations, directed primarily at systemic risk, have many connections to those of official bodies and industry groups of major industrial countries surveyed at some length in an annex to the report. These include: stronger risk management by both HLIs and their counterparties; enhanced regulatory oversight of HLIs' credit providers; further progress in industry practices with regard to such aspects as the measurement of exposures and of liquidity risk, stress testing, collateral management and external valuation, as well as in building market infrastructure in areas such as the harmonization of documentation, valuation and bankruptcy practices. In addition, the Working Group recommended fuller public disclosures by HLIs in the context of a movement towards improved and more comparable risk-based public disclosure by financial institutions more generally.

Most of these recommendations are capable of having beneficial effects on "market dynamics issues" and of reducing systemic risk. However, the Working Group limited itself to two recommendations

---

[36] One instance of such activity, which attracted much attention in 1998, was the "double play" in which some financial institutions are believed to have engaged in Hong Kong (China). This operation is described as follows in the Working Group's report (FSF, 2000c: 117): "Some market participants suggested that there were attempts to carry out a 'double play' involving the equity and currency markets, whereby short positions would be first established in the equity (or equity futures) market, and sales of Hong Kong dollars would then be used to drive up interest rates and thereby depress equity prices. Some other market participants questioned whether such a strategy was pursued. Any double play would have been facilitated at that time by institutional factors in the linked exchange rate arrangement which made short-term interest rates very sensitive to changes in the monetary base, and also by reduced market liquidity as a result of the Asian crisis. Among those taking short positions in the equity market were four large hedge funds, whose futures and options positions were equivalent to around 40 per cent of all outstanding equity futures contracts as of early August, prior to the HKMA [Hong Kong Monetary Authority] intervention (there were no limits or reporting requirements on large equity futures positions at this time). Position data suggest a correlation, albeit far from perfect, in the timing of the establishment of the short positions." See also Yam (1998).

of particular relevance to the former subject. The first recommendation aims at strengthening some kinds of surveillance of activity in financial markets at the national level with a view to identifying rising leverage and other concerns relating to market dynamics that may require preventive measures. The second aims to promote guidelines of good practice for currency trading with the support of leading market participants who would review and, as necessary, revise existing codes and guidelines in this area in the light of concerns recently expressed about trading behaviour.

Underlying the second of these two recommendations is a recognition of the absence in most emerging financial markets of guidelines and codes of conduct for trading practices, such as are issued in most major financial centres by trade associations, industry groups and committees of market participants. The recommendation is that major financial institutions should take the initiative in preparing and promoting codes and guidelines for jurisdictions where they currently do not exist. If this recommendation is to be effective, it must not only lead to industry initiatives of the kind envisaged, but also to changes in actual behaviour, even though such guidelines and codes lack legal weight.

Regarding surveillance and transparency concerning market positions, the report on HLIs is more forthcoming than that on capital flows, though the somewhat veiled character of the exposition renders the nature of the different options considered, and the Group's view on their associated pros and cons, hard to grasp precisely. The collection of aggregate high-frequency information on positions in key markets is not accepted on the grounds of feasibility, cost and difficulties in obtaining compliance.[37] National initiatives involving proactive surveillance between monetary authorities, supervisors and market participants receive greater support from the Working Group, but subject to reservations and doubts concerning such matters as the costs and

---

[37] A working group of the Committee on the Global Financial System on Transparency Regarding Aggregate Positions (the Patat Group), whose mandate was to look at what aggregate data on financial markets could be collected to enhance their efficient operation, was abolished because of its finding that "it would not be possible to obtain adequately comprehensive and timely information on a voluntary basis, and legislative solutions were deemed impractical" (White, 2000: 22).

benefits of, and international participation needed for, disclosure of information on positions in major emerging-market currencies. Some surveillance of this kind (but possibly mainly of an informal nature) presumably already exists in several countries, since it would appear to have been the source of part of the information contained in the report's survey of the experience of HLIs' operations in six jurisdictions. The strongest reservations of the report in this area concern enhanced oversight by national authorities of the provision of local currency, which is necessary for the settlement of the great majority of speculative positions against a currency. These reservations are due primarily to the Working Group's view that formal procedures for this purpose constitute capital controls.

The unavoidable conclusion regarding the Working Group's recommendations on "market dynamics issues" is that they fall well short of symmetry. Although they recognize the concerns recently expressed about HLIs' practices in this area as legitimate, they devote much more attention to the obligations for transparency sought from economic actors in developing and transition economies as part of international financial reform.

Asymmetries in the assessment procedures associated with the standards initiatives are also exemplified in another report of the FSF (2000d), that of its Working Group on Offshore Financial Centres (OFCs).[38] In the context of international financial reform, there is concern that, although OFCs do not seem to have been a major cause of systemic problems so far, they might become so in the future. This is because of the growth in the assets, liabilities and off-balance-sheet activities of institutions based in OFCs, as well as growing interbank

---

[38] As the report notes (FSF, 2000d: 9), OFCs are not easily defined, but can be characterized as jurisdictions that attract a high level of non-resident activity. Traditionally, the term has implied some or all of the following: low or no taxes on business or investment income; no withholding taxes; light and flexible incorporation and licensing regimes; light and flexible supervisory regimes; flexible use of trusts and other special corporate vehicles; no requirement for financial institutions and/or corporate structures to have a physical presence; an inappropriately high level of client confidentiality based on impenetrable secrecy laws; and unavailability of similar incentives to residents. Since OFCs generally target non-residents, their business substantially exceeds domestic business. The funds on the books of most OFC banks are invested in the major international money-centre markets.

relations. In particular, the fear is that OFCs could prove an important source of contagion. The terms of reference of the Working Group included a general stock-taking of the use made of OFCs, and, more particularly, a review of their progress in enforcing international prudential and disclosure standards, and in complying with international agreements on the exchange of supervisory information and other information relevant to combating financial fraud and money laundering.

For this purpose, the Working Group organized a survey of OFCs that aimed at assessing compliance with the international standards of supervision established by the BCBS, the IAIS and IOSCO (i.e., with standards for the banking, insurance and securities business). The survey was conducted through two questionnaires – one for onshore supervisors in 30 major financial centres and the other for 37 OFCs. The first questionnaire was designed to elicit views on the quality of regulation and supervision in those OFCs with which the onshore supervisors had some degree of familiarity, and on the quality of cooperation they had experienced with OFC supervisors. The second questionnaire was intended to provide information on how these OFCs interacted with the home supervisors of suppliers of financial services operating in or from their jurisdictions (i.e., branches, subsidiaries or affiliates of suppliers incorporated in an onshore jurisdiction). The survey was the basis of a classification of OFCs into three groups: (i) those generally viewed as cooperative, with a high quality of supervision, which largely adhered to international standards; (ii) those generally seen as having procedures for supervision and cooperation in place, but where actual performance fell below international standards and there was substantial room for improvement; (iii) those generally seen as having a low quality of supervision or being non-cooperative with onshore supervisors (or both), and as making little or no attempt to adhere to international standards. However, several supervisors in OFCs considered that the procedures followed in this exercise had provided them with an inadequate opportunity for self-assessment of their regulatory regimes and of the quality of their supervision. Providing OFCs with such an opportunity would have been in better accord with the spirit of the report's proposals concerning the future programme for assessment of standards implementation on the part of OFCs. One of the stages specified is self-assessment assisted by external supervisory expertise (FSF, 2000d: 56-60). As a class, OFCs do not arouse much sympathy within the international community. However, smooth progress in global initiatives on standards requires a perception of even-handedness regarding different aspects of their application among all the parties involved.[39]

D. IMPLEMENTATION, SANCTIONS AND INCENTIVES

Implementation of standards is a process with several dimensions and stages. The first step specified in the strategy of the FSF Task Force (FSF, 2000a, sect. III) is to identify and achieve international consensus on standards. This is followed by a prioritization exercise so that the process of implementation becomes manageable – an exercise which has led to the list of key standards in table 1. Action plans at the national level then need to be drawn up. The primary agents involved here are national governments, which consult multilateral financial institutions and standard-setting bodies as necessary and can receive technical assistance of various kinds. Once implementation of plans is under way, it is subject to assessment, partly by the relevant national authorities themselves, but also by multilateral financial institutions, standard-setting bodies and possibly other parties; technical assistance is also provided under this heading. Another integral part of the process of implementation is the dissemination of information on progress, in particular, to market participants such as lenders and investors.

---

[39] The point was eloquently expressed in a recent editorial in the periodical, *The Financial Regulator*, as follows: "The interconnection of the world financial system has created ... problematic externalities, with ... small countries now able to do a lot of damage. With world government some way off, these externalities are likely to prove tricky to manage. For the foreseeable future there is no better solution than international cooperation. When big countries push little countries around, even for the best of reasons, they give this crucial cooperation a bad name. The challenge for those interested in global financial stability is to find some way of negotiating better regulation while avoiding ... the heavy-handedness characterizing the current drive against offshore centres." See "Justice for offshore centres", *The Financial Regulator*, September 2000.

Box 1

BASEL CAPITAL STANDARDS

THE Basel Capital Accord of 1988 was the result of an initiative to develop more internationally uniform prudential standards for the capital required for banks' credit risks. The objectives of the Accord were to strengthen the international banking system and to promote convergence of national capital standards, thus removing competitive inequalities among banks resulting from differences on this front. The key features of this Accord were a common measure of qualifying capital, a common framework for the valuation of bank assets in accordance with their associated credit risks (including those classified as off-balance-sheet), and a minimum level of capital determined by a ratio of 8 per cent of qualifying capital to aggregate risk-weighted assets. In subsequent years, a series of amendments and interpretations were issued concerning various parts of the Accord. These extended the definition and purview of qualifying capital, recognized the reductions in risk exposure which could be achieved by bilateral netting meeting certain conditions, interpreted the Accord's application to multilateral netting schemes, allowed for the effects on risk exposure of collateralization with securities issued by selected OECD public-sector entities, and reduced the risk weights for exposures to regulated securities firms. Simultaneously, the Basel Committee continued its work on other banking risks, of which the main practical outcome so far has been the amendment of the 1988 Accord to cover market risk, which was adopted in 1996. The 1988 Basel Accord was designed to apply to the internationally active banks of member countries of the Basel Committee on Banking Supervision, but its impact was rapidly felt more widely; by 1999 it formed part of the regime of prudential regulation not only for international but also for strictly domestic banks in more than 100 countries.

From its inception, the 1988 Basel Accord was the subject of criticism directed at such features as its failure to make adequate allowance for the degree of reduction in risk exposure achievable through diversification, the possibility that it would lead banks to restrict their lending, and its arbitrary and undifferentiated calibration of certain credit risks. In the case of country risk, with very limited exceptions this calibration distinguished only between OECD and non-OECD countries – a feature of the Accord which some developing countries considered unjustifiably discriminatory. In the aftermath of the financial crises of the 1990s, the Accord's contribution to financial stability more generally became a focus of attention. There was special concern here with regard to the incentives which the Accord's risk weighting was capable of providing to short-term interbank lending – a significant element of the volatile capital movements during these crises.

The Basel Committee responded by initiating a comprehensive overhaul of the 1988 Accord. Its first proposal for this purpose (*A New Capital Adequacy Framework* – henceforth New Framework), published in June 1999 (BCBS, 1999b), incorporates three main elements or "pillars": (i) minimum capital rules based on weights that are intended to be more closely connected to credit risk than those of the 1988 Accord; (ii) supervisory review of capital adequacy in accordance with specified qualitative principles; and (iii) market discipline based on the provision of reliable and timely information. In early 2001 (as *TDR 2001* was completed), a revised set of proposals was issued that is designed to take account of comments by the banking industry and supervisors around the world.

The New Framework contains two basic approaches to the numerical standards for capital adequacy: the standardized and the internal-ratings-based approaches. A major feature of the standardized approach is the proposal for recourse to the ratings of credit-rating agencies in setting weights for credit risk. The New Framework's proposal regarding the internal-ratings-based approach is still tentative and will require adequate safeguards concerning such matters as the calibration of risk and comparability. However, the approach is likely to be an option in the revised proposals for banks with sufficiently sophisticated systems for handling credit risk.

The New Framework's proposal for recourse to the ratings of credit-rating agencies in setting weights for credit risk has proved highly contentious. Perhaps most importantly, there is a widespread view that the track record of the major agencies, especially with

limited importance, and it will, therefore, have a correspondingly low weight in their lending and investment decisions.

E.   STANDARDS, FINANCIAL REGIMES AND FINANCIAL STABILITY

As already mentioned, the improvements described in previous sections will entail extensive changes for many countries, and their implementation could be lengthy. This is particularly true of the required reforms in the legal and regulatory framework and of their incorporation into the norms of business practice, which is a prerequisite for receiving the full benefit of these reforms. The gradual and difficult nature of this process for developing and transition economies should not be taken as a reflection on their legislative and administrative competence or their political will. For example, the process of deregulating financial sectors in OECD countries or of putting in place a single-market regime in the EU for the banking and securities business – both processes involving obstacles and constraints similar to those confronting the global regimes of financial standards – took decades.[46]

The limits on the efficacy of enhanced standards and associated legal and regulatory reforms reflect various factors. One of these is the rootedness of standards in past experience, which makes them less than perfect for dealing with the consequences of innovation. Moreover, many of the standards covered by recent initiatives are directed at the behaviour of economic agents and the functioning of firms and markets. Stronger foundations at this level can reduce – but not eliminate – the likelihood and magnitude of systemic instability. Malpractice and fraud may become easier to detect as standards are enhanced, but they will not disappear. The collapse of Barings in early 1995 is an example of the broader destabilizing potential of events originating in malpractice within a single firm. More importantly,

---

[46] Deregulation of interest rates in major OECD countries, for example, has taken from seven to more than 20 years in all but a small minority of cases. The establishment of a single market for financial services in the EU took more than 30 years (Cornford and Brandon, 1999: 11-13).

systemic crises in the financial sector are often closely linked to macroeconomic dynamics and to developments at the international level – or regional level within a country – which transcend particular national financial sectors. A Utopian vision of standards might include standards for macroeconomic policy designed to put an end to phenomena such as boom-bust cycles, which historically have frequently proved to be the financial sector's nemesis. But, as already noted in subsection B.1, the codes of good practices regarding various aspects of macroeconomic policy in table 1 concern transparency and procedural issues, and not the contents of such policy itself.

The crucial field of banking supervision illustrates the limitations of standards. A natural starting-point here is the licensing of banks. In some countries the relevant criteria were long designed primarily to ensure adequate levels of competence and integrity among those owning and controlling a bank. But licensing is often also used to serve less limited objectives, such as the avoidance of "overbanking", limitation of financial conglomeration, and (in the case of foreign entities) restricting foreign ownership of the banking sector, or ensuring that the parent institution is adequately supervised in its home country. The objectives of licensing may have (usually proximate) relations to banking stability, but they cannot prevent serious banking instability or banking crises. Another major subject of banking supervision is implementation of prudential regulation, much of which is concerned with ensuring adequate management and internal controls, but which also includes prudential capital requirements.[47] A key purpose of capital here is to provide a stable resource to absorb any losses incurred by an institution, and thus protect the interests of its depositors. Capital requirements for credit and market risks are also clearly intended to contribute to financial risk management of assets and liabilities, as well as to appropriate pricing of the different products and services which a bank offers. Prudential capital, by strengthening financial firms, reduces the likelihood of major financial instability originating in the failure of a single firm. It also

---

[47] Capital requirements are attributed a central role in countries' regimes of prudential regulation and supervision. They have also been the subject of major international initiatives, of which the most important is the Basel Capital Accord that is currently undergoing a major revision. See box 1 on Basel Capital Standards.

increases such firms' defences against instability originating else-where. However, its contribution to restraining financial instability stops here. Other prudential guidelines or rules are directed at subjects such as exposure to foreign-exchange risks, risks due to large expo-sures to single counterparties or groups of related counterparties, adequate liquidity, loan-loss provisions, consolidated financial report-ing and country exposures. These guidelines and rules serve the same objectives as prudential capital, and their efficacy is subject to the same limitations.

These limitations are explicable, at least in part, in terms of the considerations raised above concerning standards more generally. Financial regulation is constantly struggling to keep up with financial innovation, and in this struggle it is not always successful. There is thus a continuing danger that new practices or transactions, not yet ad-equately covered by the regulatory framework, may prove a source of financial instability. Closely related in many ways to financial innova-tion are difficulties – which have become more important in recent years – regarding the transparency required for regulation and super-vision. The balance sheets of many financial firms have an increas-ingly chameleon-like quality which reduces the value of their financial returns to regulators. Consequently, the tensions between financial innovation and effective regulation in modern financial markets are unlikely to disappear. In principle, one can envisage a tightening of regulation sufficiently drastic as to come close to eliminating the dangers due to innovation. However, the tightening would be too stifling to be politically acceptable in any country that values dyna-mism in its financial sector.

Probably the most important determinant of the intrinsic limita-tions of regulation and supervision is the unavoidable dependence of financial stability on macroeconomic stability more generally.[48] Most assets of banks are susceptible to changes in their quality resulting from broader changes in economic conditions. So long as cycles of financial boom and bust are features of the economic system, so also

---

[48] This dependence, of course, provides the link between sectoral policies aimed at financial stability and macroeconomic policies, including those directed at the balance of payments (amongst which, especially for developing and transition economies, should be counted controls on capital transactions).

will be unforeseeable deteriorations in the status of many bank assets.[49] Where banking crises are combined with currency crises, and cross-border as well as domestic financing contributes to the boom (as in many recent instances involving developing economies), the process is fuelled by forces similar to those that characterize purely domestic credit cycles. These include herd behaviour of lenders and investors, driven partly by the very conditions their lending and investment have helped to create, but also by competition within the financial sector. Other forces include the all-too-ready acceptance, for example, of benchmarks resulting from collective behaviour, poor credit evaluation (often exacerbated in the case of cross-border financing by less familiarity with the borrowers and their economies), and the pressures on loan officers resulting from target returns on capital. An important distinctive feature of boom-bust cycles with a cross-border dimension is another macroeconomic factor – the exchange rate. Capital inflows generally come in the first place in response to exchange-rate adjusted returns, and thus on assumptions about the stability of the exchange rate. The outflows are in most cases associated with movements in contradiction with these assumptions, in the form of a large depreciation of the currency. This often has devastating effects on the net indebtedness and income of many domestic economic actors.

In thinking about the interaction between broader types of financial instability and difficulty in controlling financial risks, as experienced in the internal controls of banks as well as in their supervision, the concept of "latent concentration risk" (used in some recent literature on credit risk to denote problems due to unpredictable correlations between defaults) can be an illuminating one. This concept also serves to pinpoint relations between uncertainty, on the one hand, and the limitations of banking supervision, on the other.[50] Concentration risk is traditionally handled in the context of banking regulation and supervision through limits on the size of exposures to particular borrowers. For this purpose, "borrower" is typically defined

---

[49] The argument here follows closely that of Akyüz and Cornford (1999: 30-31). See also *TDR 1998* (Part One, chap. IV, sect. C.3).
[50] See, for example, Caouette, Altman and Narayanan (1998: 91, 240). The limitations of credit risk models in handling correlations among defaults are reviewed in BCBS (1999c, Part II, sect. 6, and Part III, sect. 3).

mates, almost two-thirds of emerging-market economies were using intermediate exchange rate regimes in 1991, but by 1999 this proportion had fallen to 42 per cent, and the proportion using hard pegs or some variant of floating had risen to 58 per cent (Fischer, 2001, fig. 2). However, while many countries afflicted by financial crisis in the past decade have subsequently adopted floating rates, the increased volatility associated with such regimes has become a source of concern. As a result, there now appears to be a greater interest among developing countries and transition economies in hard pegs. And increasingly, in a closely integrated global financial system, the existence of many independent currencies is being called into question (Hausmann, 1999).

For emerging-market economies, adjustable peg regimes are problematic under free capital mobility as they lead to boom-bust cycles and overshooting of exchange rates. However, neither free floating nor hard pegs constitute viable alternatives. Currency misalignments and gyrations associated with floating regimes can have serious consequences for developing countries with small and open economies and a relatively large stock of external debt denominated in reserve currencies. On the other hand, for most developing countries and transition economies, a policy of locking into a reserve currency and surrendering monetary policy autonomy can entail considerable costs in terms of growth, employment and international competitiveness – costs that far exceed the benefits such a regime may yield in terms of price and exchange rate stability. These conclusions are shared in a paper on exchange rate regimes for emerging-market economies jointly prepared by staff of the French and Japanese Ministries of Finance, on the occasion of the meeting of European and Asian finance ministers in Kobe, Japan, in January 2001:

> There is no guarantee that currency board arrangements escape from the same drawbacks as pegged regimes. ... Free-floating strategies have their own costs of possible excessive volatility and free riding risks. (Ministry of Finance, Japan, 2001: 3-4)

A consequence of the mainstream advice is that developing countries with similar foreign trade structures and market orientation could end up at opposite ends of the spectrum of exchange rates – some with floating and others with fixed exchange rates against the dollar – even if there is a considerable amount of trade amongst them. Consequently, not only would their currencies be floating against each other, but also their bilateral exchange rates would be greatly influenced by the overall movement of the dollar against other currencies. Given the misalignments and fluctuations that characterize the currency markets, this would imply erratic, unexpected shifts in the competitive position of developing countries *vis-a-vis* each other. When there is considerable bilateral trade, as between Brazil and Argentina, such shifts can have an important impact on their economies, leading to tensions in trade relations. Briefly stated, unilateral corner solutions may result in inconsistent outcomes for the developing countries taken together.

The key question is whether there exists a viable and appropriate exchange rate regime for developing and transition economies that are closely integrated into global financial markets when major reserve currencies are subject to frequent gyrations and misalignments, and when the size and speed of international capital movements can very quickly overwhelm the authorities in such countries and narrow their policy options. Can these countries be expected to solve their exchange rate problems unilaterally when the magnitude, direction and terms and conditions of capital flows are greatly influenced by policies in major reserve-currency countries, and when international currency and financial markets are dominated by speculative and herd behaviour? Certainly, controls over capital flows can facilitate the prudent management of their exchange rates. Indeed, a few countries, such as China, have so far been able to pursue adjustable peg regimes without running into serious problems. However, several emerging markets have already made a political choice in favour of close integration into the global financial system and are unwilling to control capital flows. Furthermore, it may be very difficult for any single country to resist the strong trend towards liberalization of capital movements, particularly if it has close links with international markets through foreign direct investment (FDI) and trade flows.

While all this implies that the solution should, in principle, be sought at the global level, the prospects for this are not very promising, given the stance of the major powers on the question of exchange rates. Since global arrangements for a stable system of exchange rates are not foreseeable in the near future, the question arises as to whether viable solutions can be found at the regional level. In this respect, the post-Bretton Woods experience of Europe in establishing mechanisms to achieve a stable pattern of intraregional exchange rates, and eventually move to a currency union, may hold useful lessons for developing regions, particularly East Asia and South America. However, while regional currency arrangements and monetary cooperation among developing countries could bring some benefits, they do not resolve the problem of what currency regime to adopt and how to achieve exchange rate stability *vis-a-vis* G-3 currencies. Even if they could achieve greater integration, developing countries could not neglect their exchange rates *vis-a-vis* such currencies. It thus appears that regional arrangements among developing countries may need to involve major reserve-currency countries or rely on a common regime of capital controls in order to achieve stability and avoid costly crises.

B. EXCHANGE RATE REGIMES

1. Soft pegs

It has long been established that an economy which is fully committed to free movement of capital (or which does not succeed in effectively controlling capital movements) cannot both fix its exchange rate (at a given value or within a narrow band) and pursue an independent monetary policy. Any attempt to do so will eventually run into inconsistencies that will force the country to abandon one of the objectives. One option would be to adhere to fixed exchange rates through currency boards or outright dollarization at the expense of autonomy in monetary policy. Another would be to move to floating exchange rates, thereby freeing monetary policy from defending a particular exchange rate (or a narrow band). The breakdown of the Bretton Woods system of adjustable pegs, the 1992-1993 crisis in the Exchange Rate Mechanism (ERM) of the European Monetary System (EMS) and the recent episodes of crisis in emerging markets are all seen as the outcome of the inconsistency between capital account openness, exchange rate targeting and independent monetary policy.

The Bretton Woods system of adjustable pegs operated with

widespread controls over international capital movements. However, inconsistencies between the pattern of exchange rates and the domestic policy stances of major countries created serious payments imbalances and incentives for capital to move across borders, circumventing the controls. This eventually led to the breakdown of the system and the adoption of floating rates. Even though the adjustable pegs in the EMS constituted a step towards monetary union (hard pegs) and were supported by extensive intraregional monetary cooperation, inconsistencies between macroeconomic fundamentals and exchange rates led to a crisis and breakdown of the ERM in 1992-1993.The adoption of soft pegs is also considered to be one of the root causes of recent financial crises in emerging-market economies such as Mexico, Thailand, Indonesia, the Republic of Korea, the Russian Federation and Brazil. The subsequent move by these countries to floating rates is often interpreted as the recognition that soft pegs are not viable for countries closely integrated into the global financial markets.

The role of soft pegs in contributing to external fragility and the outbreak of financial crises in emerging markets is well established.[2] Most emerging-market economies offer higher nominal interest rates than the industrialized world, in large part because of higher inflation rates. These create short-term arbitrage opportunities for international investors and lenders, as well as incentives for domestic firms to reduce their costs of finance by borrowing abroad. On the other hand, by providing implicit guarantees to international debtors and creditors, currency pegs can encourage imprudent lending and borrowing. The risk of depreciation is discounted owing to the stability of the nominal exchange rate and the confidence created by rapid liberalization and opening up of the economy. The credibility of the peg as well as arbitrage opportunities are enhanced when the country pursues a tight monetary policy in order to bring down inflation or prevent overheating of the economy.

However, a nominal peg with a higher inflation rate also causes an appreciation of the currency in real terms and a widening of the current-account deficit. If external deficits and liabilities are allowed

---

[2]   For an earlier account of this process, before the recent surge in capital flows to emerging markets, see *TDR 1991* (Part Two, chap. III, sect. F); *TDR 1998* (Part One, chap. III, sect. B); and *TDR 1999* (Part Two, chap. VI).

to mount, the currency risk will rise rapidly. Since there is no firm commitment to defend the peg, the worsening fundamentals eventually give rise to expectations of a devaluation and a rapid exit of capital. Not only does this cause liquidity shortages; it also forces the monetary authorities to tighten monetary policy and restrict liquidity even further. Sooner or later, the exchange rate peg is abandoned, leading to a free fall which, together with the hike in interest rates, causes enormous dislocation in the economy.

Despite the risk of costly currency swings and crises, many countries with relatively high rates of inflation have often favoured stabilizing the internal value of their currencies by stabilizing their external value through anchoring to a reserve currency with a good record of stability. This is true not only for the small and open European economies such as Austria, the Netherlands and Belgium, but even for a large economy such as Italy, which faced several speculative attacks against its currency and experienced disruptions throughout the process of convergence towards the inflation rates of its larger trading partners in the EU. Many emerging-market economies, notably in Latin America, have also used soft pegs for disinflation. Although it proved difficult to achieve an orderly exit from such pegs in order to realign their currencies, it is notable that these countries managed to avoid the return of rapid inflation in the aftermath of crises, despite sharp declines in their currencies. For instance, after the introduction of an exchange-based stabilization plan (*Plano Real*) in 1994, Brazil succeeded in bringing down its inflation rate from a four-digit level to a single-digit level by 1998. Despite various adjustments in the value of the real and a relatively rapid decline in inflation, the Brazilian currency had appreciated by some 20 per cent at the end of the disinflation process. However, it was not possible to engineer an orderly realignment of the exchange rate, which came under severe pressure at the end of 1998, partly due to spillovers from the Russian crisis. But after an initial hike, inflation stabilized at low levels despite a sharp drop in the value of the real against the dollar (*TDR 1999*, Part One, chap. III, sect. B).

Appreciation is generally unavoidable in exchange-based stabilization programmes because of stickiness of domestic prices. More fundamentally, it is part of the rationale of successful disinflation, since greater exposure to international trade – resulting in lower import prices and increased competition in export markets – helps to discipline domestic producers and acts as a break on income claims. However, such programmes are often launched without adequate attention to the potential problems of real currency appreciation and without a clear exit strategy (i.e., when and how to alter the peg and/ or the regime and realign the exchange rate). Although economically it may appear simple to restore international competitiveness by a one-off adjustment in the exchange rate, this solution may be politically difficult. Indeed, problems in finding a political solution tend to be underestimated. Governments are often unwilling to abandon the peg and devalue after exerting considerable effort in attempting to convince people that the fixed rate has brought them more good than harm. They are also afraid of losing markets' confidence and facing a sharp reversal of capital flows and a collapse of their currency.

Given the herd behaviour of financial markets, such fears of a hard landing are not always unfounded, even though, as noted above, sharp currency declines rarely result in the return of rapid inflation. Forewarning an exit strategy is risky, since it is not always easy to judge how rapidly inflation will decline. The Turkish exchange-based stabilization programme of December 1999 had such a strategy. However, it failed to meet its inflation target and, after a series of economic and political crises, the government was obliged to abandon the peg and move to the other corner, floating, before the preannounced exit date (*TDR 2001*, chap. II, box 2.1). In Europe, institutional arrangements in the context of the EMS that involved assistance from anchor countries have helped, on several occasions, to engineer necessary adjustments in the currencies of the pegging countries without leading to instability and contagion (see below). However, such arrangements are not easily replicable for emerging markets that peg unilaterally. Support from international financial institutions could help achieve orderly exits, but the experience so far has not been very encouraging.[3]

---

[3] For instance, the 1998 Brazilian programme with the IMF had stipulated an orderly exit from the peg through gradual devaluations throughout 1999, as well as emergency financing, but this did not prevent the crisis.

Soft pegs are not used only for disinflation. In East Asia, for example, exchange rate stability was an important ingredient of the export-oriented development strategy of the individual economies and was intended to support the regional division of labour in the context of the "flying-geese" process. Because of the concentration of Asian exports in dollar-denominated markets, nominal exchange rates in the region, although not fixed, had been kept generally stable within a band of around 10 per cent in relation to the dollar since the late 1980s. Given their low inflation rates, in most East Asian economies the appreciation of the currency was moderate or negligible. The combination of stable nominal exchange rates, rapid economic growth and relatively high nominal interest rates inspired confidence and attracted international investors and lenders. However, this led to a build-up of considerable currency risks and external financial fragility, resulting eventually in a rapid exit of capital, with spillover effects throughout the region through herd behaviour. Even in Indonesia, orderly currency adjustment was not possible despite sound macroeconomic fundamentals and the timely action taken by the government to widen the currency band in order to stop contagious speculation (*TDR 1998*, Part One, chap. III; Akyüz, 2000).

One way out of these problems is to use controls over capital flows while maintaining a soft peg. Taxes and reserve requirements on inflows designed to remove short-term arbitrage opportunities can help preserve monetary autonomy, and a policy of high interest rates can be pursued without encouraging speculative capital inflows and a build-up of excessive currency risk. However, as long as domestic inflation is high, currency appreciation cannot be avoided. This is particularly serious when currency pegs are used for disinflation. In any case, a large majority of developing countries have been unwilling to impose controls on capital inflows during the boom phase of the financial cycle as a means of deterring short-term arbitrage flows, for the same reasons that they were unwilling to exit from pegged exchange rates after successful disinflation. Again, as explained in the next chapter, they are even less willing to impose controls over capital outflows in order to stabilize exchange rates and free monetary policy from pressures in the currency markets at times of speculative attacks and crisis.

2. Floating

Does free floating constitute a viable alternative for developing countries and transition economies? Can such countries really leave the external value of their currencies to the whims of international capital flows and dedicate monetary policy entirely to domestic objectives such as price stability or full employment? To what extent would such objectives be undermined by excessive volatility and misalignments associated with free floating?

Quite apart from how appropriate such a regime might be, for a number of reasons it is particularly unsuitable for developing countries and transition economies, as well as for smaller industrial countries. Compared to the major industrial economies, developing and emerging-market economies are much more dependent on foreign trade, which is typically invoiced in foreign currencies. On average, the share of international trade in their domestic production is twice as large as in the United States, the EU or Japan, so that the impact of exchange rate movements on their domestic economic conditions – including prices, production and employment – is much greater. Moreover, these economies have higher net external indebtedness, a larger proportion of which is denominated in foreign currencies. Consequently, sharp changes in their exchange rate tend to generate debt servicing difficulties, and liquidity and solvency problems. In sharp contrast, a country such as the United States can borrow in its own currency, therefore effectively passing the exchange rate risk onto creditors.[4]

It is also argued that most developing and transition economies lack credible institutions, and this in itself is a cause of greater volatility in market sentiment and exchange rates, which is believed to have led to a widespread "fear of floating" among emerging markets. Consequently, a large number of those countries which claim to allow

---

[4] This inability of a country to borrow in its own currency has been coined the "original sin hypothesis" (Hausmann, 1999; Eichengreen and Hausmann, 1999). A corollary of this hypothesis is that "... the country's aggregate net foreign exposure must be unhedged, by definition. To assume the ability to hedge is equivalent to assume that countries can borrow abroad in their own currencies but choose not to do so, in spite of the fact that the market does not appear to exist" (Eichengreen and Hausmann, 1999: 25).

their exchange rates to float actually pursue intermediate regimes, and use interest rates and currency-market intervention to influence exchange rates. This finding also contradicts the claim that emerging markets have been moving away from adjustable peg regimes (Calvo and Reinhart, 2000; Fischer, 2001; Reinhart, 2000).

The experience of major industrial countries with floating rates during the interwar years as well as since the breakdown of the Bretton Woods system suggests that volatility, gyrations and misalignments in exchange rates cannot simply be attributed to lack of credible institutions. Rather, they are systemic features of currency markets dominated by short-term arbitrage flows. The French experience in the 1920s, for example, was lucidly described in a report of the League of Nations in 1944:

> The dangers of such cumulative and self-aggravating movements under a regime of freely fluctuating exchanges are clearly demonstrated by the French experience of 1922-26. Exchange rates in such circumstances are bound to become highly unstable, and the influence of psychological factors may at times be overwhelming. French economists were so much impressed by this experience that they developed a special "psychological theory" of exchange fluctuations, stressing the indeterminate character of exchange rates when left to find their own level in a market swayed by speculative anticipations ... The experience of the French franc from 1922 to 1926 and of such interludes of uncontrolled fluctuations as occurred in certain currencies in the 'thirties demonstrates not only the difficulty of maintaining a freely fluctuating exchange on an even keel, ... it also shows how difficult it may be for a country's trade balance to adjust itself to wide and violent variations. (League of Nations, 1944: 118, 119)

Writing in 1937 about the same experience, von Hayek explained gyrations not only in terms of short-term capital flows; he also argued that floating rates encouraged such capital flows:

> It is because ... the movements of short-term funds are frequently due, not to changes in the demand for capital for investment, but to changes in the demand for cash as liquidity reserves, that short-

term international capital movements have such a bad reputation as causes of monetary disturbances. And this reputation is not altogether undeserved. ... I am altogether unable to see why under a regime of variable exchanges the volume of short-term capital movements should be anything but greater. Every suspicion that exchange rates were likely to change in the near future would create an additional powerful motive for shifting funds from the country whose currency was likely to fall or to the country whose currency was likely to rise ... This means that if the original cause is already a short-term capital movement, the variability of exchanges will tend to multiply its magnitude and may turn what originally might have been a minor inconvenience into a major disturbance. (von Hayek, 1937: 62-64)

As discussed in some detail in earlier UNCTAD *TDRs*, since the breakdown of the Bretton Woods arrangements, volatility, persistent misalignments and gyrations have also been the dominant features of the exchange rates of the major reserve currencies.[5] Despite a significant convergence of inflation rates and trends in unit labour costs during the past decade, the G-3 exchange rates have continued to show persistent misalignments and large gyrations. Such disorderly behaviour has caused serious problems for developing countries in the management of their currencies and external debt, and has often been an important factor in major emerging-market crises. But these problems have generally been ignored by the major industrial countries which, for the most part, have geared their monetary policy to domestic objectives, notably combating inflation. Only on a few occasions have the United States and Japan, for example, which are committed to free floating, resorted to intervention and ad hoc policy coordination when currency instability and misalignments posed serious threats to their economic prospects – in the second half of the 1980s, in order to realign and stabilize the dollar in the face of mounting protectionist pressures

---

[5]   For an assessment of the experience in the 1980s, see UNCTAD secretariat (1987); Akyüz and Dell (1987); and also *TDR 1990* (Part Two, chap. I). For the more recent experience, see *TDR 1993* (Part Two, chap. I); *TDR 1994* (Part Two, chap. II); *TDR 1995* (Part Two, chap. I); *TDR 1996* (Part Two, chap. I); and *TDR 1999* (chap. III).

associated with large trade imbalances, and again in the mid-1990s, when the yen rose to unprecedented levels against the dollar.

Developing countries are encouraged to adopt floating on the grounds that the resulting exchange rate uncertainty would remove implicit guarantees and discourage imprudent lending and borrowing. However, experience shows that crises are as likely to occur under floating rates as under adjustable pegs (World Bank, 1998). Under financial liberalization and free capital mobility, nominal exchange rates fail to move in an orderly way to adjust to differences in inflation rates (i.e., the purchasing power parity is not preserved), while adjustment of interest rates to inflation is quite rapid. As a result, currencies of high-inflation countries tend to appreciate over the short term. Under soft pegs, excessive capital inflows (i.e., inflows in excess of current-account needs) attracted by arbitrage opportunities would increase international reserves, while under floating, they would lead to nominal appreciations, which reinforce – rather than temper – capital inflows and aggravate the loss of competitiveness caused by high inflation. Although appreciations also heighten currency risks, markets can ignore them when they are driven by herd behaviour. For instance, if the currencies in East Asia had been allowed to float in the early 1990s, when inflows were in excess of current-account needs, the result could have been further appreciations and widening payments imbalances. Indeed, in the face of such large capital inflows during the early 1990s, many governments in East Asia generally chose to intervene in order to prevent appreciation (*TDR 1998*, box 2).

As already noted, the post-war experience of emerging markets with floating is rather limited; it is largely concentrated in the aftermath of recent episodes of financial crisis. Nevertheless, it reveals a number of features that belie the promises of its advocates. In Latin America, for instance, domestic interest rates have been more sensitive to changes in United States rates, and more variable in countries with floating regimes than those with fixed or pegged rates, implying less – rather than more – monetary autonomy and greater risk to the financial system (Hausmann, 1999). Floating appears to promote procyclical monetary policies as interest rates tend to rise during recession. It also leads to the shrinking of domestic financial markets and to high interest rates by increasing the risk of holding domestic assets.

3.   Hard pegs

It thus appears that emerging-market economies with open capital accounts cannot achieve sustained economic and financial stability by either pegging or floating their currencies. There remain the options of hard pegs, currency boards or outright dollarization. At the end of the 1990s, the currencies of 45 economies, members of the IMF, had hard pegs, of which 37 (including the then 11 euro-currency countries) had no independent legal tender, and the remainder (including Argentina, Hong Kong (China) and the transition economies of Bulgaria, Estonia and Lithuania) had currency boards (Fischer, 2001). With the exception of the European Monetary Union (EMU), most economies without an independent legal tender were small. More recently, Ecuador and El Salvador have adopted the dollar as their national currency and Guatemala is in the process of doing so.

Such regimes are considered particularly appropriate for countries with a long history of monetary disorder, rapid inflation and lack of fiscal discipline (i.e., where there is "exceptional distrust of discretionary monetary policy") (Eichengreen, 1999: 109). They effectively imply abolishing the central bank and discarding discretionary monetary policy and the function of lender of last resort. Not only do they remove the nominal exchange rate as an instrument of external adjustment, but also they subordinate all other policy objectives to that of maintaining a fixed nominal exchange rate or dollarization. However, these same features also provide the credibility needed for the success of such regimes since they imply that governments are prepared to be disciplined by external forces, particularly by a foreign central bank with a record of credible monetary policy. The expected economic benefits include low inflation, low and stable interest rates, low cost of external borrowing and, if there is outright dollarization, the ability to borrow abroad in the currency circulated domestically. Furthermore, dollarization is expected to deepen the financial sector, extend the maturities of domestic financial assets and encourage long-term financing. It is often favoured by private business in emerging markets because it increases predictability and reduces the cost of transactions.

Some of these benefits can be significant. For a small economy which is closely integrated with, and dependent on, a large reserve-

Historically, exits from currency boards have occurred in the context of decolonization, when the pound sterling was often the anchor currency. Unlike their modern counterparts, the rationale for establishing such regimes was not to gain credibility; rather, they were imposed by the colonial power with a view to reinforcing trade ties with its colonies. In principle, by retaining a national currency, currency board regimes – as distinct from dollarization – allow for devaluation and even exit. However, there is no modern currency board regime with a known exit strategy; indeed, making such a strategy known would defeat its very purpose. For this reason, an orderly exit from a currency board regime is unlikely to be possible, especially when the economic costs of adhesion militate in favour of change. By contrast, when the regime works well, governments feel no need for exit.

C. REGIONAL ARRANGEMENTS: THE EUROPEAN EXPERIENCE

Given the difficulties that developing countries have been facing in finding unilateral solutions to the problem of managing their currencies and preventing financial crises, and given the resistance of the major powers to genuine reform of the international financial architecture, attention has increasingly focused on regional solutions (Chang, 2000; Mistry, 1999; Park and Wang, 2000). In this context, there is growing interest in the lessons provided by the European experience with regional monetary cooperation and currency arrangements in the post-Bretton Woods era, which culminated in a monetary union at the end of the 1990s.

The first response of Europe to the collapse of the Bretton Woods system in the early 1970s consisted of "snake" and "snake in the tunnel" arrangements that were designed to stabilize the intra-European exchange rates within relatively narrow bands in an environment of extreme volatility. This was followed by the creation of the EMS in 1979 with the participation of the members of the European Economic Community (EEC), and eventually by the introduction of the euro and the establishment of the EMU in 1999.[7] Thus it took some 30 years to pass from soft pegs to hard pegs.

After the collapse of the Bretton Woods system, European countries were able to avoid inflationary spillovers from the United States by appreciation of their currencies *vis-a-vis* the dollar, and floating against the dollar was seen as consistent with their objective of stabilizing the internal value of their currencies. However, given the relatively high degree of regional integration, a move towards free floating among the European currencies posed a potential threat of instability and disruptions to intraregional trade and resource allocation, particularly for small and open economies. A policy of establishing a stable pattern of intraregional exchange rates and collectively floating against the dollar was seen as an appropriate solution, since the trade of the region as a whole with the rest of the world was relatively small. In effect, regional integration and monetary cooperation was designed to establish Europe as a single large economy – like that of the United States – with limited dependence on international (extra-European) trade.

Although the decision to join such arrangements (or, in the Austrian view, to "tie their own hands" in monetary affairs) was taken unilaterally by each country, the system that emerged involved multi-

---

[7] The first major political initiative for a European monetary union was taken in 1969 with the adoption of the Werner Report, which proposed: for the first stage, a reduction of the fluctuation margins between the currencies of the member states of the Community; for the second stage, the achievement of complete freedom of capital movements, with integration of financial markets; and for the final stage, an irrevocable fixing of exchange rates between the currencies. In its first effort at creating a zone of currency stability, the EEC attempted in 1971 to fix European parities closer to each other than to the dollar, but with some flexibility ("the snake"). The "snake" rapidly died with the collapse of the dollar-based Bretton Woods system, but was reborn in 1972 as the "snake in the tunnel", a system which narrowed the fluctuation margins between the Community currencies (the snake) in relation to those operating between these currencies and the dollar (the tunnel). During the currency turmoil that accompanied the 1973 oil crisis, this arrangement could not function well, leading to various exits and floating, until the establishment of the EMS in 1979. The United Kingdom was a member of the EMS but did not participate in the ERM until 1990. For the history of European monetary integration and the functioning of the EMS, see Bofinger and Flassbeck (2000).

lateral commitments at the regional level. Since the deutschemark had been the most stable currency after the war and Germany was the largest market in the region, the German currency provided a natural anchor for many European countries following the collapse of the Bretton Woods arrangements. Given the political will of the participating countries to move towards greater integration, Germany did not simply provide an anchor currency; it also assumed responsibilities *vis-a-vis* the anchoring countries in securing the stability of the arrangements through such means as intervention in the currency markets and provision of lender-of-last-resort financing, although the latter role has never been explicitly stated. As for the smaller countries, although they sacrificed part of their monetary autonomy, they were considerably strengthened *vis-a-vis* currency markets and became less dependent on international financial institutions.

In the process leading to a common currency, the adjustable pegs adopted were crucially different from the unilateral soft pegs used by emerging markets in recent years in that both anchoring and anchor countries shared the common objective of achieving monetary convergence and internal and external stability for their currencies. The system was also designed to reduce one-way bets, which might have been encouraged by inflation and interest rate differentials, by establishing bands around the so-called "parity grids". It established obligations for symmetric interventions as well as unlimited short-term credit facilities among central banks designed to maintain bilateral exchange rates within the band. It also made available to member countries various types of external payments support to enable ERM participants both to keep their currencies within prescribed fluctuation limits and to cope with circumstances that might threaten orderly conditions in the market for a member country's currency.[8] In addition, it stipulated concrete procedures for realignment of the bands. Furthermore, European integration allowed special arrangements in the ERM

---

[8]   For a useful survey of mechanisms for external payments support in the EEC, see Edwards (1985: 326-346). As part of the establishment of the Economic and Monetary Union, the European Monetary Cooperation Fund – the body which administered short-term facilities under the heading of mutual external financial support – was dissolved and its functions taken over by the European Monetary Institute (EMI).

for the less advanced countries – Greece, Ireland, Portugal and Spain – including the provision of considerable fiscal compensation, which did much to enable them to achieve monetary and fiscal convergence and meet the EMU stability criteria.

These arrangements were also supported by a European Community regime for capital movements, which, until a directive in 1988, provided governments with some leeway for restricting different categories of transaction, along with some liberalization obligations which were less stringent for short-term and potentially speculative transactions. The 1988 directive abolished restrictions on capital movements between residents of European Community countries, subject to provisos concerning the right to control short-term movements during periods of financial strain.[9] The directive also stated that European Community countries should endeavour to attain the same degree of liberalization of capital movements *vis-a-vis* third countries as among themselves. However, governments retained the right to take protective measures with regard to certain capital transactions in response to disruptive short-term capital movements. Upon adoption of the single currency, such measures could be taken only in respect of capital movements to or from third countries.

Despite the establishment of institutions to support the exchange rate arrangements and integration, the path to monetary union has not been smooth; it has often been disrupted by shocks and policy mistakes. In some instances disruptions were similar to currency crises experienced by emerging markets under soft pegs. As in emerging markets, occasionally pressures developed as a result of differences in the underlying inflation rates: at the high end of the inflation spectrum was Italy (and subsequently the United Kingdom), followed by France with moderate inflation, while Germany and Austria were at the lower end. For high-inflation countries, therefore, currency realignments were needed from time to time until their inflation rates converged towards that of the anchor country. On many occasions inflation differentials were widened by external or internal shocks which, in effect, tested the resilience of the system and the commitments of the

---

[9]   In addition, there was an obligation to take the measures necessary for the proper functioning of systems of taxation, prudential supervision, etc. For more details, see Akyüz and Cornford (1995).

imposing discipline, because the underlying fundamentals of the French economy were as strong as those in Germany. This experience shows that, just as with unilateral pegging or fixing, regional currency arrangements, even with supporting institutions, can run into trouble in the absence of appropriate policy actions to bring exchange rates into conformity with underlying fundamentals. Again, while it is true that the hegemony of an anchor country in regional arrangements is balanced by responsibilities that are not present in unilateral pegging or fixing, policies pursued by such a country may still turn out to be too restrictive for other members. Indeed, tight German monetary policy appears to have been a factor in the speculative attack on the French franc during the EMS crisis.

With the move to a single currency, smaller members of the EMU are expected to exert a somewhat greater influence on the common monetary policy. Furthermore, strong trade linkages can be a force for stability and convergence, with expanding economies providing additional demand and export markets for those members experiencing a downturn. Even though asymmetric shocks and structural differences may still produce significant divergence of economic performance among countries at different levels of development, such differences do not need to cause serious policy dilemmas if countries are prepared to use the various instruments they still have at their disposal. However, under certain circumstances, the constraints imposed on fiscal policy by the Stability and Growth Pact could impair the ability to smooth out intraregional differences in economic performance.

D.   OPTIONS FOR DEVELOPING COUNTRIES: DOLLARIZATION OR REGIONALIZATION?

Despite the temporary setbacks in 1992-1993, and shortcomings in the design of policies and institutional arrangements which constrained policy options, European monetary cooperation has been successful in securing stability in intraregional exchange rates, containing financial contagion and dealing with fluctuations *vis-a-vis* the dollar and the yen. To what extent can such arrangements be replicated by developing countries as a means of collective defence against systemic instability? Is it feasible for developing countries to establish regional arrangements among themselves without involving G-3 countries, and to follow a path similar to that pursued by Europe – from a regionally secured exchange rate band to a currency union? Alternatively, could they go directly to currency union by adopting a regional currency?

Interest in regional monetary arrangements and cooperation in the developing world has increased rapidly since the outbreak of the Asian crisis. For example, at the 1997 Annual Meetings of the IMF and the World Bank, soon after the outbreak of the crisis, a proposal was made to establish an Asian Monetary Fund. Subsequently, an initiative was launched in May 2000 involving swap and repurchase arrangements among member countries of the Association of South-East Asian Nations (ASEAN), China, Japan and the Republic of Korea (see box 3). More recently, the joint French-Japanese paper cited in section A above (Ministry of Finance, Japan, 2001: 5-6) has given support to the strengthening of regional cooperation in East Asia, drawing on the European experience:

> Strengthened regional cooperation is a way of ensuring both stability and flexibility ... The European Monetary Union process provides a useful example of how further integration can be achieved ... In this regard, an important step was taken in Chiang Mai on 6 May 2000 to establish a regional financial arrangement to supplement existing international facilities ... Regional co-operation frameworks should be fully integrated into the overall monetary and financial system.

Interest has also been expressed in establishing regional currencies, as opposed to dollarization, in Latin America. A recent statement made by the President of the Inter-American Development Bank stated:

> The issue (of dollarization) is very controversial and has both its defenders and detractors, but we do not think the conditions are appropriate in most countries for taking that route ... We believe, however, that the important conditions are in place for thinking about sub-regional currencies. (Reported in *SUNS*, 11 January 2000.)

Box 2

REGIONAL MONETARY AND FINANCIAL
COOPERATION AMONG DEVELOPING COUNTRIES

AT present there are few regional financial and monetary arrangements among developing countries, apart from those in East Asia described in box 3. Such arrangements as do exist range from agreements to pool foreign exchange reserves, such as the Andean Reserve Fund and the Arab Monetary Fund, to currency pegging (Rand Monetary Area) and a regional currency (Eastern Caribbean Monetary Union). The Communauté financiere africaine (CFA) also has a common currency, but is unique in that it involves an agreement between its members and a major European country on cooperation in monetary and exchange-rate policy.

The *Andean Reserve Fund* was established in 1976 by the members of the Andean Community – Bolivia, Colombia, Ecuador, Peru and Venezuela – and has a subscribed capital of $2 billion. The Fund provides financial support to its members in the form of loans or guarantees for balance-of-payments support, short-term (liquidity) loans, emergency loans, loans to support public external debt restructuring, and export credit. Conditionality for drawing on these facilities is softer than that of the IMF. The Fund also aims at contributing to the harmonization of the exchange-rate, monetary and financial policies of member countries. It is thus intended to promote economic and financial stability in the region and to further the integration process in Latin America.[1]

The *Arab Monetary Fund* was established in 1976 with a structure similar to that of the IMF and comprises all members of the League of Arab States (except the Comoros). It has a subscribed capital of 326,500 Arab accounting dinars, equivalent to about $1.3 billion. The Fund aims at promoting exchange-rate stability among Arab currencies and at rendering them mutually convertible, and it provides financial support for members that encounter balance-of-

---

[1]   For more detailed information, see FLAR (2000).

payments problems. It is also intended to serve as an instrument to enhance monetary policy cooperation among members and to coordinate their policies in dealing with international financial and economic problems. Its final aim is to promote the establishment of a common currency.

In the *Rand Monetary Area*, Lesotho and Swaziland, both economically closely integrated with South Africa, peg their currencies to the South African rand without formally engaging in coordination of monetary policy.

The *Eastern Caribbean Monetary Union* is an arrangement for a common currency among the members of the Organization of Eastern Caribbean States, a group of small island developing countries.[2] The currency is pegged to the dollar, but in contrast to France with respect to the CFA (see below), the United States does not play an active role in the pegging arrangement.

The creation of the *Communauté financiere africaine* goes back to 1948, but the agreements governing the current operation of the CFA zone were signed in 1973. There are two regional groups, each with its own central bank: the Economic and Monetary Union of West Africa, and the Central African Economic and Monetary Community.[3] The 14 countries involved have a common currency, the CFA franc, that is not traded on the foreign exchange markets but is convertible with the French franc at a fixed parity. There is free capital mobility within the CFA zone, and between these countries and France, and the foreign exchange reserves of

---

[2]   The member states are Antigua and Barbuda; Dominica; Grenada; Montserrat; St Kitts and Nevis; Saint Lucia; and St Vincent and the Grenadines. The British Virgin Islands and Anguilla are associate members.

[3]   The Economic and Monetary Union of West Africa comprises Benin, Burkina Faso, Cote d'Ivoire, Guinea-Bissau, Mali, Niger, Senegal and Togo; and the Central African Economic and Monetary Community comprises Cameroon, Central African Republic, Chad, Congo, Equatorial Guinea and Gabon. The two groups maintain separate currencies, but since both have the same parity with the French franc, they are subject to the same regulatory framework. And because there is free capital mobility between each of the two regions, the CFA franc zone can be considered as a single currency area. The Comoros has a similar arrangement but maintains its own central bank.

If established and sustained, regional currencies among developing-country groupings can bring considerable benefits, similar to those expected from the introduction of the euro. They can reduce transaction costs of doing business within a region and eliminate exchange rate spreads and commissions in currency trading associated with intraregional trade and investment. For example, such effects are estimated to raise the combined GDP of the euro area by some 0.5 per cent. The adoption of the euro is also expected to raise intraregional trade, primarily through trade diversion (*TDR 1999*, Part One, chap. III). Furthermore, a supranational central bank can reduce the influence of populist national politics on monetary policy, while nevertheless being accountable to member countries. Unlike dollarization, such an arrangement would also bring benefits in terms of seigniorage (Sachs and Larrain, 1999: 89).

Establishing regional arrangements – including regional currencies – among developing countries would also reduce the likelihood of asynchronous cycles and asymmetric shocks to the extent that there are similarities in their economic structures and institutions. In other words, a grouping of developing countries alone is more likely to meet the conditions of an optimal currency area than one which also involves developed countries.

However, in drawing lessons from Europe for developing countries, it is necessary to take into account certain differences between the two. The European experience shows that small and highly open economies with close regional trade links can establish and sustain a system of stable exchange rates around a major reserve currency so long as there are clear guidelines regarding the maintenance and alteration of members' currency bands, appropriate allocation of responsibilities and supporting institutions and policies. Such arrangements can be operated for quite a long time without major disruptions and can help to deepen integration (see box 2). For larger groups and for countries of equal size or economic power, however, there could be significant difficulties in establishing and sustaining such systems. There would be an additional difficulty when the group does not contain a major reserve-currency country.

Consequently, unless they are organized around a major reserve-currency country, developing countries of comparable size may find it difficult to form a group to establish and sustain ERM-type currency grids and ensure that the monetary and financial policies pursued independently by each country are mutually compatible and consistent with the stability of exchange rates. Moreover, without the involvement of a large reserve-currency country, it could be difficult to put in place effective defence mechanisms against speculative attacks on individual currencies. Under these conditions, while a rapid move to monetary union through the adoption of a regional currency might be considered desirable, it would face similar problems of implementation as the introduction of an exchange rate mechanism. Recognition of such difficulties and adoption of appropriate mechanisms to overcome them are essential if developing countries are to succeed in their attempts to form regional monetary groupings aimed at attaining greater exchange rate and financial stability.

The absence of a major reserve-currency country in regional arrangements also poses problems of credibility. It may be especially difficult for countries with a long history of monetary disorder and inflation to form a credible monetary union without involving a major reserve-currency country with a good record of monetary discipline and stability. In this regard, Latin America is clearly less favourably placed than East Asia.

More fundamentally, for developing countries to manage on their own regional exchange rates *vis-a-vis* the G-3 currencies is a daunting task, whether it is undertaken within the framework of a monetary union or under ERM-type arrangements. They cannot simply float their currencies and adopt an attitude of benign neglect towards the value of their currencies *vis-a-vis* the rest of the world, even under conditions of deep regional integration. For instance, in East Asia, while intraregional trade among the countries of the region (ASEAN, first-tier newly industrializing economies (NIEs) and China) is important and constantly growing, it still accounts for less than half of their total trade (*TDR 1996*, Part Two, chap. I, sect. E), compared to two-thirds in the EU. Furthermore, as a proportion of GDP, the trade of East Asian developing countries with the rest of the world is more than twice as large as that of the United States, the EU or Japan. Accordingly, their exchange rates *vis-a-vis* G-3 currencies can exert a considerable influence on their economic performance. Furthermore, regional arrangements would not protect them against financial shocks, since they carry large stocks of external debt in G-3 currencies.

Box 3

THE CHIANG MAI INITIATIVE

EVEN before the financial crisis of 1997, there had been a growing interest in East Asia in pursuing regional policy coordination and monetary cooperation. Various swap arrangements and repurchase agreements had been introduced, and these initiatives intensified during the Mexican crisis in the mid-1990s. However, none of these moves prepared the region for the currency runs of 1997 and 1998.

In a Joint Statement on East Asia Cooperation issued at the summit of "ASEAN plus 3" (the 10 members of ASEAN plus China, Japan and the Republic of Korea) in November 1999, it was agreed to "strengthen policy dialogue, coordination and collaboration on the financial, monetary and fiscal issues of common interest" (Ministry of Finance, Japan, 2000a: 8). Against this background, the region's Finance Ministers launched the so-called "Chiang Mai Initiative" in May 2000, aimed at building networks for multilayered financial cooperation to match the growing economic interdependence of Asian countries and the consequently greater risk that financial shocks could lead to regional contagion.[1] The Initiative envisages the use of the ASEAN+3 framework to improve exchange of information on capital flows and to launch moves towards the establishment of a regional economic and financial monitoring system. The core of the Initiative is a financing arrangement among the 13 countries that would strengthen the mechanism of intraregional support against currency runs. This arrangement, building on the previous ASEAN Swap Arrangement (ASA), is intended to supplement

---

[1]   For further information on the Initiative, see Ministry of Foreign Affairs of the Kingdom of Thailand (2000); Ministry of Finance, Japan (2000a and 2000b); "Asia finance: Central banks swap notes", *The Economist*, 16 May 2000.

existing international financial cooperation mechanisms. It is also expected to contribute to the stability of exchange rates within the region.

The previous ASA, which dates back to 1977, comprised only five countries (Indonesia, Malaysia, the Philippines, Singapore and Thailand). Total funds committed under the arrangement were $200 million – a negligible amount compared to the combined loss of foreign exchange reserves of $17 billion that the five countries experienced between June and August 1997.

The new ASA envisaged under the Chiang Mai Initative includes Brunei Darussalam and allows for the gradual accession of the four remaining ASEAN countries (Cambodia, Lao People's Democratic Republic, Myanmar and Vietnam). But its most important element is the inclusion of bilateral swap and repurchase arrangements between the ASEAN countries and China, Japan and the Republic of Korea. Funds available under the new ASA total $1 billion. However, the commitments of the three non-ASEAN countries to the bilateral swap arrangements are likely to be substantially greater than this; they will be determined by the level of their foreign currency reserves and the amounts that were involved in earlier agreements between Japan and the Republic of Korea ($5 billion) and Japan and Malaysia ($2.5 billion). The conditions for drawing on the facilities and a number of technicalities remain to be agreed in negotiations among the countries concerned, but it appears that assistance under the bilateral swap arrangements will, in principle, be linked to IMF support (Ministry of Finance, Japan, 2000b).

These factors thus render floating against G-3 currencies unattractive and raise the question of what constitutes an appropriate exchange rate regime at the regional level. One option is to establish a crawling band, with the central rate defined in terms of a basket of G-3 currencies.[10] The joint French-Japanese paper cited above suggested that such an intermediate regime could be a possible step towards monetary union:

> A possible solution for many emerging-market economies could be a managed floating exchange rate regime whereby the currency moves within a given implicit or explicit band with its centre targeted to a basket of currencies. ... managed free-floating exchange rate regimes may be accompanied for some time, in certain circumstances, by market-based regulatory measures to curb excessive capital inflows. (Ministry of Finance, Japan, 2001: 3-4)

The paper went on to argue that a "group of countries with close trade and financial links should adopt a mechanism that automatically moves the region's exchange rates in the same direction by similar percentages". This would imply fixed bands for currencies of members, as in the ERM. But as the European experience shows, there would also be a need to alter such bands in line with changes in inflation rates, for example. Such a regime, pursued collectively, may need to be supported by a collective system of control over capital movements. For reasons already mentioned, control over capital flows – both inward and outward – can be more easily agreed upon when countries act together rather than separately. In such an arrangement, intraregional capital flows may be deregulated – as in the EMU – but capital flows to and from non-member countries would have to be controlled – as in the formative years of the EMS – in order to restrict short-term, potentially destabilizing movements.

Any regional monetary arrangement would need to include mechanisms to support the regional currency, or currencies, in order to keep exchange rates in line with targets and stem speculative attacks. Since the East Asian crisis, various proposals have been put

---

[10]   Such a regime is coined BBC (basket, band and crawl) (Williamson, 2000).

forward to establish regional support mechanisms for intervention in currency markets and for the provision of international liquidity to countries facing a rapid exit of capital. The 1997 proposal to establish an Asian facility of $100 billion was "derailed quickly by the United States Treasury and IMF for fear that it would detract from the role (and power) of the latter and make it even more difficult to get the United States' contribution to the IMF's latest quota increase authorized by the United States Congress" (Mistry, 1999: 108).[11] Another proposal made was to pool and deploy national reserves to defend currencies facing speculative attacks and to provide international liquidity to countries without the stringent conditions typically attached to such lending by international financial institutions. For instance, on the eve of the Thai crisis in 1997, the combined net reserves of East Asia – including Japan – exceeded $500 billion, and by 2000 had risen to about $800 billion (Park and Wang, 2000). Pooling of reserves can also be supplemented by regional agreements to borrow among regional central banks, modelled on the IMF's General Arrangements to Borrow (GAB), as recently proposed by Singapore as a form of mutual assistance.

Arrangements such as pooling of national reserves or swap facilities among central banks can undoubtedly do much to stabilize exchange rates, even when they involve only developing countries of the region. However, they are likely to be more effective in smoothing out short-term volatility and responding to isolated currency pressures than in stalling systemic crises. Given the herd behaviour of financial markets, the speed of spillovers and extent of contagion, it may be impossible to sustain an ERM-type currency band at times of crisis simply by drawing on a pool of national reserves, if there is no possibility of recourse to a regional lender of last resort. Besides, maintaining a high level of reserves for this purpose would be a very expensive way of securing insurance against financial panics. As discussed in the next chapter, a more viable alternative would be to resort to unilateral standstills and exchange and capital controls at times of speculative attacks.

---

[11] This source also provides a detailed discussion of other proposals for regional arrangements.

In a world of systemic and global financial instability, any regional arrangement designed to achieve exchange rate stability in order to prevent crises, and manage them better if they nonetheless occur, should also incorporate a number of other mechanisms, with the aim of ensuring enhanced regional surveillance, information-sharing and early warning. Domestic reforms would still be needed in many of the areas discussed in the previous chapter in order to provide a sound basis for regional cooperation. Just as domestic policy actions without appropriate global arrangements would not be sufficient to ensure greater financial stability, regional arrangements could fail in the absence of sound domestic institutions and policies.

As European experience has shown, progress towards a currency union can be a long and drawn-out process, requiring political will and a "culture" of regionalism. Regional monetary arrangements linking several national currencies through exchange rate bands can encounter serious problems even when there are supporting institutions. It would not be easy for developing countries to replicate the European experience, with or without the help of G-3 countries. However, the threat of virulent financial crises, together with the lack of genuine progress in the reform of the international financial architecture, has created a sense of urgency in emerging markets, notably in East Asia, for building collective defence mechanisms at the regional level. In this context, recent initiatives and proposals, however modest they may be, constitute an important step forward.

REFERENCES

Akyüz Y (2000). Causes and sources of the East Asian financial crisis. Paper presented at the Host Country Event: Symposium on Economic and Financial Recovery in Asia, UNCTAD X, Bangkok, 12 February.

Akyüz Y and Cornford A (1995). International capital movements: some proposals for reform. In: Michie J and Grieve Smith J, eds. *Managing the Global Economy*. Oxford, Oxford University Press.

Akyüz Y and Dell S (1987). Issues in international monetary reform. In: UNCTAD, *International Monetary and Financial Issues for the Developing Countries*. United Nations publication, sales no. E.87.II.D.3. New York.

Banque de France (1997). La zone franc. Note d'information no. 106. Paris.

Bofinger P and Flassbeck H (2000). The European monetary system (1979-1988). Achievements, flaws and applicability to other regions of the world. Mimeo. Geneva, UNCTAD.

Calvo G and Reinhart CM (2000). Fear of Floating. NBER Working Paper, 7993. Cambridge, MA, National Bureau of Economic Research, November.

Chang R (2000). Regional monetary arrangements for developing countries. Paper prepared for the G-24 Workshop on Coherence or Dissonance in the International Institutional Framework, Vienna, September.

Chang R and Velasco A (1998). The Asian liquidity crisis. NBER Working Paper, 6796. Cambridge, MA, National Bureau of Economic Research, November.

Clément JAP (1996). Aftermath of the CFA franc devaluation. IMF Occasional Paper, 138. Washington, DC, International Monetary Fund, May.

Edwards RW (1985). *International Monetary Collaboration*. Dobbs Ferry, NY: Transnational Publishers.

Eichengreen B (1999). *Toward a New International Financial Architecture*. Washington, DC, Institute for International Economics.

Eichengreen B and Hausmann R (1999). Exchange rates and financial fragility. NBER Working Paper, 7418. Cambridge, MA, National Bureau of Economic Research, November.

Fischer S (2001). *Exchange Rate Regimes: Is the Bipolar View Correct?* New Orleans, American Economic Association, January.

FLAR (Fondo Latinoamericano de Reservas) (2000). *Achievements and Prospects* (www.flar.net/englishv/index2.html).

Friedman M (1953). *Essays in Positive Economics,* Chicago, University of Chicago Press.

Hadjimichael MT and Galy M (1997). The CFA franc zone and the EMU. IMF Working Paper WP/97/156. Washington, DC, November.

Hausmann R (1999). Should there be five currencies or one hundred and five? *Foreign Policy,* fall.

von Hayek FA (1937). *Monetary Nationalism and International Stability* (1971 reprint of first edition). New York, Augustus M Kelley.

International Financial Institutions Advisory Commission (IFIC) (2000). Report (*"Meltzer Report"*). Washington, DC, March.

League of Nations (1944). *International Currency Experience – Lessons of the Inter-War Period*. Princeton, Princeton University Press.

McKinnon RI (1963). Optimum currency areas. *American Economic Review*, 53.

Ministry of Finance, Japan (2000a). The road to the revival of the Asian economy and financial system (www.mof.go.jp/english/i/if022g.htm).

Ministry of Finance, Japan (2000b). Announcement of 24 November 2000 (www.mof.go.jp/jouhou/kokkin/kaigi006.htm) (in Japanese).

Ministry of Finance, Japan (2001). Exchange rate regimes for emerging market economies. Discussion Paper prepared by staff of the French and Japanese Ministries of Finance. Tokyo, 16 January (www.mof.go.jp/english/asem).

Ministry of Foreign Affairs of the Kingdom of Thailand (2000). The Chiang Mai Initiative. Discussion Paper. Special ASEAN Finance Deputies Meeting (AFDM) +3, Bangkok.

Mistry PS (1999). Coping with financial crises: are regional arrangements the missing link? In: UNCTAD, *International Monetary and Financial Issues for the 1990s*. Vol. X. United Nations publication, sales no. E.99.II.D.25. New York and Geneva.

Park YC and Wang Y (2000). Reforming the international financial system: Prospects for regional financial cooperation in East Asia. In: Teunissen JJ, ed. *Reforming the International Financial System. Crisis Prevention and Response*. The Hague, FONDAD.

Reinhart C (2000). The mirage of floating exchange rates. *American Economic Review, Papers and Proceedings*, May.

Sachs J and Larrain F (1999). Why dollarization is more straightjacket than salvation. *Foreign Policy*, fall.

Summers LH (2000). International financial crises: causes, prevention and cures. *American Economic Review, Papers and Proceedings*, May.

TDR (various years). *Trade and Development Report*. United Nations sales publication. New York and Geneva, United Nations Conference on Trade and Development.

UNCTAD secretariat (1987). The exchange rate system. In: UNCTAD, *International Monetary and Financial Issues for the Developing Countries*. United Nations publication, sales no. E.87.II.D.3. New York.

Williamson J (2000). Exchange rate regimes for emerging markets: Reviving the intermediate option. Washington, DC, Institute of International Economics, September.

World Bank (1998). *Global Development Finance*. Washington, DC.

Chapter 4

Crisis Management and Burden Sharing

Yılmaz Akyüz

A. INTRODUCTION

THERE is a growing body of opinion that effective management of financial crises in emerging markets requires a judicious combination of action on three fronts: a domestic macroeconomic policy response, particularly through monetary and fiscal measures and exchange rate adjustment; timely and adequate provision of international liquidity with appropriate conditionality; and the involvement of the private sector, especially international creditors. With the benefit of hindsight, it is now agreed that the international policy response to the Asian crisis was far from optimal, at least during the initial phase. An undue burden was placed on domestic policies; rather than restoring confidence and stabilizing markets, hikes in interest rates and fiscal austerity served to deepen the recession and aggravate the financial problems of private debtors. The international rescue packages were designed not so much to protect currencies against speculative attacks or finance imports as to meet the demands of creditors and maintain an open capital account. Rather than involving private creditors in the management and resolution of the crises, international intervention, coordinated by the IMF, in effect served to bail them out.[1]

This form of intervention is increasingly considered objectionable on grounds of moral hazard and equity. It is seen as preventing

---

[1] For an analysis of the policy response to the Asian crisis, see *TDR 1998* (chap. III); and *TDR 2000* (chap. IV).

market discipline and encouraging imprudent lending, since private creditors are paid off with official money and not made to bear the consequences of the risks they take. Even when the external debt is owed by the private sector, the burden ultimately falls on taxpayers in the debtor country, because governments are often obliged to serve as guarantors. At the same time, the funds required for such interventions have been getting ever larger and are now reaching the limits of political acceptability. Thus, a major objective of private sector involvement in crisis resolution is to redress the balance of burden sharing between official and private creditors as well as between debtors and creditors.

For these reasons, the issues of private sector involvement and provision of official assistance in crisis management and resolution have been high on the agenda in the debate on reform of the international financial architecture since the outbreak of the East Asian crisis. However, despite prolonged deliberations and a proliferation of meetings and forums, the international community has not been able to reach agreement on how to involve the private sector and how best to design official lending in financial crises. As acknowledged by the IMF, "While some success has been achieved in securing concerted private sector involvement, it has become increasingly clear that the international community does not have at its disposal the full range of tools that would be needed to assure a reasonably orderly – and timely – involvement of the private sector" (IMF, 2000a: 10). This chapter seeks to address this problem by defining the state of play, examining the issues that remain to be resolved and assessing various options proposed.

B.   PRIVATE SECTOR INVOLVEMENT AND ORDERLY DEBT WORKOUTS

Private sector involvement in financial crisis resolution refers to the continued or increased exposure of international creditors to a debtor country facing serious difficulties in meeting its external financial obligations, as well as to arrangements that alter the terms and conditions of such exposure, including maturity rollovers and debt write-offs.[2] In this context, it is useful to make a distinction between mechanisms designed to prevent panics and self-fulfilling debt runs, on the one hand, and those designed to share the burden of a crisis between debtors and creditors, on the other. To the extent that private sector involvement would help restrain asset grabbing, it would also reduce the burden to be shared. For instance, debt standstills and rollovers can prevent a liquidity crisis from translating into widespread insolvencies and defaults by helping to stabilize the currency and interest rates. In this sense, private sector involvement in financial crises is not always a zero-sum game. It can also help resolve conflict of interest among creditors themselves by ensuring more equitable treatment.

Market protagonists often argue that foreign investors almost always pay their fair share of the burden of financial crises in emerging markets. According to this view, international banks incur losses as a result of arrears and bankruptcies, while holders of international bonds suffer because the financial difficulties of the debtors affect the market value of bonds, and most private investors mark their positions to market (Buchheit, 1999: 6). Losses incurred in domestic bond and equity markets are also cited as examples of burden sharing by private investors.[3]

In assessing creditor losses, it is important to bear in mind that, so long as the value of claims on the debtor remains unchanged, mark-to-market losses may involve only a redistribution among investors. On the other hand, net losses by creditors are often compensated by risk spreads on lending to emerging markets. For instance, on the eve of the Asian crisis, the total bank debt of emerging markets was close to $800 billion. Applying a modest 300 basis points as the average spread on these loans would yield a sum of more than $20 billion per

---

[2]   A wider use of the concept includes greater transparency in standards of policy-making and improved data dissemination, as these measures are seen to be essential for markets to appropriately assess and price risks (IMF, 2000b, chap. V).
[3]   According to the Institute for International Finance, losses incurred by private investors since 1997 in emerging-market crises have amounted to $240 billion for equity investors, $60 billion for international banks and $50 billion for other private creditors on a mark-to-market basis (Haldane, 1999: 190). Losses incurred by foreign banks in the Asian crisis are estimated at some $20 billion (Zonis and Wilkin, 2000: 96).

annum in risk premium, compared to the estimated total mark-to-market losses[4] of foreign banks of some $60 billion incurred in emerging-market crises since 1997.

Foreign investors are directly involved in burden sharing when their claims are denominated in the currency of the debtor country and they rush to exit. This hurts them twice, by triggering sharp drops both in asset prices and in the value of the domestic currency. For this reason, countries that borrow in their own currencies (or adopt a reserve currency as their own) are expected to be less prone to currency and debt crises since potential losses would deter rapid exit and speculative attacks.

However, the denomination of external debt in the currency of the debtor country does not eliminate the so-called collective action problem which underlines self-fulfilling debt runs and provides the principal rationale for debt standstills; even though creditors as a group are better off if they maintain their exposure, individual investors have an incentive to exit quickly for fear of others doing so before them. The consequent declines in domestic asset prices and in the value of the currency not only hurt creditors, but also have serious repercussions for the debtor economy. In some cases, there could be a run for the strong foreign-owned domestic banks as well, placing a particular burden on locally-owned and smaller banks and other financial institutions. It is for these reasons that governments of debtor countries are often compelled to take action to prevent a rapid exit of foreign investors from domestic capital markets. Such actions may go beyond monetary tightening. In Mexico, for instance, market pressures in 1994 forced the government to shift from peso-denominated *cetes* to dollar-indexed *tesebonos* in the hope that removing the currency risks would persuade foreign creditors to stay. However, this did not prevent the eventual rush to exit, the collapse of the peso and hikes in interest rates. Thus, even when external debt is denominated in domestic currency, arrangements to involve private creditors through standstills and rollovers can play an important role in efforts to achieve greater financial stability.

---

[4]   Losses resulting from daily adjustments to reflect current market value, as opposed to historic accounting (or both) value.

As discussed in detail in *TDR 1998*, the rationale and key principles for an orderly debt workout can be found in domestic bankruptcy procedures. Although Chapter 11 of the United States Bankruptcy Code is the most cited reference, other major industrial countries apply similar principles. These principles combine three key elements: (i) provisions for an automatic standstill on debt servicing that prevents a "grab race" for assets among the creditors; (ii) maintaining the debtor's access to the working capital required for the continuation of its operations (i.e., lending into arrears); and (iii) an arrangement for the reorganization of the debtor's assets and liabilities, including debt rollover, extension of existing loans, and debt write-off or conversion. The way these elements are combined depends on the particularities of each case, but the aim is to share the adjustment burden between debtor and creditors and to assure an equitable distribution of the costs among creditors.

Under these procedures, standstills give the debtor the "breathing space" required to formulate a debt reorganization plan. While, in principle, agreement is sought from creditors for restructuring debt, the procedures also make provisions to discourage holdouts by allowing for majority – rather than unanimous – approval of the creditors for the reorganization plan. The bankruptcy court acts as a neutral umpire and facilitator, and when necessary has the authority to impose a binding settlement on the competing claims of the creditors and debtor under so-called "cramdown" provisions.

Naturally, the application of national bankruptcy procedures to cross-border debt involves a number of complex issues. However, fully-fledged international bankruptcy procedures would not be needed to ensure an orderly workout of international debt. The key element is internationally sanctioned mandatory standstills. Under certain circumstances, it might be possible to reach agreement on voluntary standstills with creditors but, as recognized by the IMF, "... in the face of a broad-based outflow of capital, it may be difficult to reach agreement with the relevant resident and non-resident investors ..." (IMF, 2000a: 10). On the other hand, while debtor countries have the option to impose unilateral payment suspension, without a statutory basis such action can create considerable uncertainties, thereby reducing the likelihood of orderly debt workouts. Furthermore, debtors could be deterred from applying temporary payment standstills for fear of litigation and asset seizure by creditors, as well as of lasting adverse effects on their reputation.

Standstills on sovereign debt involve suspension of payments by governments themselves, while on private external debt they require an imposition of temporary exchange controls which restrict payments abroad on specified transactions, including interest payments. Further restrictions may also be needed on capital transactions of residents and non-residents (such as acquisition of assets abroad or repatriation of foreign capital). Clearly, the extent to which standstills would need to be combined with such measures depends on the degree of restrictiveness of the capital account regime already in place.

Since standstills and exchange controls need to be imposed and implemented rapidly, the decision should rest with the country concerned, subject to a subsequent review by an international body. According to one proposal, the decision would need to be sanctioned by the IMF. Clearly, for the debtor to enjoy insolvency protection, it would be necessary for such a ruling to be legally enforceable in national courts. This would require a broad interpretation of Article VIII(2)(b) of the Articles of Agreement of the IMF, which could be provided either by the IMF Executive Board or through an amendment of these Articles so as to cover debt standstills. In this context, Canada has proposed an Emergency Standstill Clause to be mandated by IMF members (Department of Finance, Canada, 1998).

However, as argued in *TDR 1998*, the IMF Board is not a neutral body and cannot, therefore, be expected to act as an independent arbiter, because countries affected by its decisions are also among its shareholders. Moreover, since the Fund itself is a creditor, and acts as the authority for imposing conditionality on the borrowing countries, there can be conflicts of interest *vis-a-vis* both debtors and other creditors. An appropriate procedure would thus be to establish an independent panel for sanctioning such decisions. Such a procedure would, in important respects, be similar to GATT/WTO safeguard provisions that allow developing countries to take emergency actions when faced with balance-of-payments difficulties (see box 4).

For private borrowers the restructuring of debts should, in principle, be left to national bankruptcy procedures. However, these remain highly inadequate in most developing countries. Promoting an orderly workout of private debt, therefore, crucially depends on establishing and developing appropriate procedures. Ordinary procedures for handling individual bankruptcies may be inappropriate and difficult to apply under a more widespread crisis, and there may be a need to provide general protection to debtors when bankruptcies are of a systemic nature. One proposal that has been put forward is "... to provide quasi-automatic protection to debtors from debt increases due to a devaluation beyond a margin ..." (Miller and Stiglitz, 1999: 4). Clearly, the need for such protection will depend on the extent to which standstills and exchange controls succeed in preventing sharp declines in currencies. For sovereign debtors, it is difficult to envisage formal bankruptcy procedures at the international level, but they too could be given a certain degree of protection against debt increases brought about by currency collapses. Beyond that, negotiations between debtors and creditors appear to be the only feasible solution. As discussed below, these may be facilitated by the inclusion of various provisions in debt contracts, as well as by appropriate intervention of multilateral financial institutions.

C. RECENT DEBATE WITHIN THE IMF

Despite its potential benefits to both debtors and creditors, private sector involvement in crisis resolution has proved to be one of the most contentious issues in the debate on reform of the international financial architecture. While the international community has increasingly come to recognize that market discipline will only work if creditors bear the consequences of the risks they take, it has been unable to reach agreement on how to bring this about. According to one view, a voluntary and case-by-case approach would constitute the most effective way of involving the private sector in crisis resolution. Another view is that, for greater financial stability and equitable burden sharing, a rules-based mandatory approach is preferable. This divergence of views is not simply between debtor and creditor countries, but also among the major creditor countries.

The main argument in favour of a rules-based system is that a case-by-case approach could lead to asymmetric treatment – not only

Box 4

GATT AND GATS BALANCE-OF-PAYMENTS
PROVISIONS AND EXCHANGE RESTRICTIONS

THE balance-of-payments provisions of Articles XII and XVIIIB
of the General Agreement on Tariffs and Trade (GATT) 1994
allow a Member to suspend its obligations under the Agreement
and to impose import restrictions in order to forestall a serious
decline in, or otherwise protect the level of, its foreign exchange
reserves, or to ensure a level of reserves adequate for implementation of its programme of economic development.[1] The provisions
of Article XVIIIB (part of Article XVIII dealing with governmental assistance to economic development) are directed particularly
at payments difficulties arising mainly from a country's efforts to
expand its internal market or from instability in its terms of trade.
Permissible actions include quantitative restrictions as well as
price-based measures. In applying such restrictions, the Member
may select particular products or product groups. The decision is
taken unilaterally, with notification to the WTO Secretariat and
subsequent consultations with other Members in the Committee on
Balance-of-Payments Restrictions. Restrictions are imposed on a
temporary basis and are expected to be lifted as conditions improve. However, the Member cannot be required to remove restrictions by altering its development policy.

Similar provisions are to be found in Article XII of the
General Agreement on Trade in Services (GATS), which stipulates
that, in the event of serious difficulties in the balance of payments
and in external finance, or a threat thereof, a Member may adopt or
maintain restrictions on trade in services on which it has undertaken specific commitments, including on payments or transfers
for transactions related to such commitments. Again, such restrictions are allowed to ensure, *inter alia*, the maintenance of a level of
financial reserves adequate for implementation of the Member's

---

[1]   For more detailed discussion, see Jackson (1997, chap. 7); and Das (1999,
chap. III.3).

programme of economic development or economic transition. The conditions and modalities related to the application of such restrictions are similar to those in the GATT 1994 balance-of-payments provisions.

Clearly, these provisions are designed to avoid conditions in which countries are forced to sacrifice economic growth and development as a result of temporary difficulties originating in the current account of the balance of payments, particularly trade deficits. Even though they may not be invoked directly for the restriction of foreign exchange transactions and the imposition of temporary standstills on debt payments at times of severe payments difficulties arising from the rapid exit of capital – and a consequent capital-account crisis – resort to such action in those circumstances would be entirely in harmony with the provisions' underlying rationale.

between debtors and creditors, but also among different creditors. It would also leave considerable discretion to some major industrial powers, which have significant leverage in international financial institutions, to decide on the kind of intervention to be made in emerging-market crises. Private market actors, as well as some major industrial countries, are generally opposed to involuntary mechanisms on the grounds that they create moral hazard for debtors, that they alter the balance of negotiating strength in favour of the latter, that they delay the restoration of market access, and that they can be used to postpone the adjustments needed.[5]

The recent debate within the IMF on private sector involvement in crisis resolution appears to have focused on three mechanisms. First, it is agreed that the Fund should try, where appropriate, to act as a catalyst for lending by other creditors to a country facing payments difficulties. If this is inappropriate, or if it fails to bring in the private sector, the debtor country should seek to reach an agreement with its creditors on a voluntary standstill. Finally, it is recognized that, as a last resort, the debtor country may find it necessary to impose a unilateral standstill when voluntary agreement is not feasible. All these measures

---

[5] On the private sector position, see IIF (1999); and IMF (2000b).

should also be accompanied by appropriate monetary and fiscal tightening and exchange rate adjustment. A report of the meeting of the IMF Executive Board concerning the involvement of the private sector in the resolution of financial crises stated:

> Directors agreed that, under the suggested framework for involving the private sector, the Fund's approach would need to be a flexible one, and the complex issues involved would require the exercise of considerable judgement. ... In cases where the member's financing needs are relatively small or where, despite large financing needs, the member has good prospects of gaining market access in the near future, the combination of strong adjustment policies and Fund support should be expected to catalyze private sector involvement. In other cases, however, when an early restoration of market access on terms consistent with medium-term external sustainability is judged to be unrealistic, or where the debt burden is unsustainable, more concerted support from private creditors may be necessary, possibly including debt restructuring ...

> Directors noted that the term "standstill" covers a range of techniques for reducing net payment of debt service or net outflows of capital after a country has lost spontaneous access to international capital markets. These range from voluntary arrangements with creditors limiting net outflows of capital, to various concerted means of achieving this objective.

> Directors underscored that the approach to crisis resolution must not undermine the obligation of countries to meet their debt in full and on time. Nevertheless, they noted that, in extreme circumstances, if it is not feasible to reach agreement on a voluntary standstill, members may find it necessary, as a last resort, to impose one unilaterally. Directors noted that ... there could be a risk that this action would trigger capital outflows. They recognized that if a tightening of financial policies and appropriate exchange rate flexibility were not successful in stanching such outflows, a member would need to consider whether it might be

necessary to resort to the introduction of more comprehensive exchange or capital controls. (IMF, 2000c)[6]

Clearly, there still remains the possibility of large-scale bailout operations. Some countries apparently attempted to exclude this possibility, but could not secure consensus:

> A number of Directors favoured linking a strong presumption of a requirement for concerted private sector involvement to the level of the member's access to Fund resources. These Directors noted that a rules-based approach would give more predictability to the suggested framework for private sector involvement, while limiting the risk that large-scale financing could be used to allow the private sector to exit. Many other Directors, however, stressed that the introduction of a threshold level of access to Fund resources, above which concerted private sector involvement would be automatically required, could in some cases hinder the resumption of market access for a member with good prospects for the successful use of the catalytic approach to securing private sector involvement.

Nor has there been agreement over empowering the IMF to impose a stay on creditor litigation in order to provide statutory protection to debtors that impose temporary standstills:

> Most Directors considered that the appropriate mechanism for signalling the Fund's acceptance of a standstill imposed by a member was through a decision for the Fund to lend into arrears to private creditors ... Some Directors favoured an amendment to Article VIII, section 2(b), that would allow the Fund to provide

---

[6] Unless stated otherwise, all quotations that follow in this section are from the same source (i.e., IMF, 2000c). For a more detailed discussion, see IMF (2000a). Temporary suspension was proposed in an earlier Working Party report to the G-10: "... in certain exceptional cases, the suspension of debt payments may be a necessary part of the crisis resolution process" (Group of Ten, 1996: 3). Subsequently, it was supported by the Council on Foreign Relations Task Force (CFRTF); see CFRTF (1999).

a member with some protection against the risk of litigation through a temporary stay on creditor litigation. Other Directors did not favour such an approach, and noted that in recent cases, members' ability to reach cooperative agreements with private creditors had not been hampered by litigation.

Considerable flexibility is undoubtedly needed in handling financial crises since their form and severity can vary from country to country. However, current practices leave too much discretion to the Fund and its major shareholders in decisions regarding the timing and extent of the official financing it should provide, and under what conditions; how much private sector involvement it should require; and under what circumstances it should give support to unilateral payment standstills and capital controls. The suggested framework generally fails to meet the main concerns of debtor countries regarding burden sharing in crisis resolution and the modalities of IMF support and conditionality. Nor does it provide clear guidelines to influence the expectations and behaviours of debtors and creditors with the aim of securing greater stability.

D.   OFFICIAL ASSISTANCE, MORAL HAZARD AND BURDEN SHARING

The above discussion suggests that there is now a greater emphasis on private sector involvement when designing official assistance to countries facing financial difficulties. The elements of this strategy include the use of official money as a catalyst for private financing, lending into arrears to precipitate agreement between debtors and creditors, and making official assistance conditional on prior private sector participation. Some of these policies were, in fact, used for the resolution of the debt crisis in the 1980s, although their objectives were not always fully met. For instance, under the so-called Baker Plan, official lending to highly-indebted developing countries sought to play a catalytic role, but faced stiff opposition from commercial banks, which refused to lend to these countries. The practice of IMF lending to debtors that are in arrears on payments owed to private creditors dates back to the Brady Plan of 1989, when commercial banks were no longer willing to cooperate in restructuring Third World debt as they had made sufficient provisions and reduced their exposure to developing-country borrowers. A decision by the IMF Board in September 1998 formally acknowledged lending into arrears as part of the Fund's lending policy and extended this practice to bonds and non-bank credits in the expectation that it would help countries with Fund-approved adjustment programmes to restructure their private debt.[7]

The current emphasis on official assistance being made conditional on private sector participation includes a commitment not to lend or grant official debt relief unless private markets similarly roll over their maturing claims, lend new money or restructure their claims. This strategy, which has come to be known as "comparability of treatment", aims not only at preventing moral hazard as it pertains to private creditors, but also at ensuring an acceptable form of burden sharing between the private and official creditors. Its underlying principle is that public assistance should not be made available unless debtors get some relief from private creditors, and no class of private creditors should be exempt from burden sharing.[8] In 1999, Paris Club creditors specifically advised Pakistan to seek comparable treatment from its private bondholders by rescheduling its eurobond obligations. However, this policy does not seem to have been implemented in the case of recent official assistance to Ecuador, when the IMF did not insist that the country reach an agreement on restructuring with the holders of its Brady bonds as a precondition for official assistance (see box 5; and Eichengreen and Ruhl, 2000: 19).

Certainly, the emphasis on burden sharing and comparable treatment between private and official creditors constitutes a major advance over the debt strategies adopted in the 1980s and in the more recent emerging-market crises. During these episodes, official intervention was designed primarily to keep sovereign debtors current on

---

[7]   This was also first proposed by the G-10 Working Party: "Such lending can both signal confidence in the debtor country's policies and longer-term prospects and indicate to unpaid creditors that their interest would best be served by quickly reaching an agreement with the debtor" (Group of Ten, 1996: 3).

[8]   On the "comparability of treatment" principle and its recent application, see Buchheit (1999); De la Cruz (2000); and IMF (2000b).

Box 5

RECENT BOND RESTRUCTURING AGREEMENTS

A number of recent sovereign bond restructuring agreements have been widely hailed by the international community for their success "... in puncturing unsustainable expectations of some investors that international sovereign bonds were, in effect, immune from restructuring ..." (IMF, 2000a: 10). However, they also show that, under current institutional arrangements, there are no established mechanisms for an orderly restructuring of sovereign bonds, and that the process can be complex and tedious.[1] Success in bringing bondholders to the negotiating table does not depend on the presence of collective action clauses (CACs) in bond documents alone. A credible threat of default could be just as effective. However, even then, the debtors are not guaranteed to receive significant debt relief, particularly on a mark-to-market basis.

Pakistan restructured its international bonds at the end of 1999 without invoking the CACs present in its bonds, preferring a voluntary offer to exchange its outstanding eurobonds for a new six-year instrument, which was accepted by a majority of the bondholders. Communication problems were not serious because the bonds were held by only a few Pakistani investors. It is believed that the presence of CACs and a trustee, as well as the request of the Paris Club to extend "comparability of treatment" to eurobonds, along with a credible threat of default, played an important role in discouraging holdouts.[2] However, the terms of restructuring were quite favourable to bondholders compared to the prevailing market price, and the new bonds offered were more liquid. According to the IMF, there was a "haircut" for the creditors compared to the relative listing price but not to the relative market value, and

---

[1] On these restructuring exercises, see De la Cruz (2000); Eichengreen and Ruhl (2000); Buchheit (1999); and IMF (2000b, box 5.3).
[2] For a different view on the impact of the Paris Club's request, see Eichengreen and Ruhl (2000: 26-28).

although the initial impact of the restructuring on the debt profile of the country was somewhat positive, "by 2001 market estimates suggest that debt-service payments will be back to levels before restructuring and will be higher for the remaining life of the exchange bond" (IMF, 2000b: 137 and table 5.2).

By contrast, **Ukraine** made use of the CACs present in four of its outstanding bonds in a restructuring concluded in April 2000. Unlike Pakistan, the bonds were spread widely among retail holders, particularly in Germany, but the country managed to obtain the agreement of more than 95 per cent of the holders on the outstanding value of debt. As in Pakistan, however, this involved only the extension of principal maturities rather than relief, since reorganization was undertaken on a mark-to-market basis. Indeed, there was a net gain for creditors relative to market value (IMF, 2000b, table 5.2).

From mid-1999 **Ecuador** started having serious difficulties in making interest payments on its Brady bonds, ending up in a default in the second half of the year. As rolling over maturities would not have provided a solution, the country sought a large amount of debt reduction by offering an exchange for global bonds issued at market rates, but with a 20-year maturity period. This was rejected by the bondholders, who furthermore voted for acceleration. After a number of failed attempts, Ecuador invited eight of the larger institutional holders of its bonds to join a Consultative Group, with the aim of providing a formal mechanism of communication with bondholders rather than negotiating terms for an exchange offer. In mid-August, bondholders accepted Ecuador's offer to exchange defaulted Brady bonds for 30-year global bonds at a 40 per cent reduction in principal, while the market discount was over 60 per cent. This resulted in a net gain for the creditors relative to market value.[3]

---

[3] For an assessment of the Ecuadorian restructuring, see Acosta (2000).

debt servicing to private creditors and the seniority accorded to multilateral debt went unchallenged. However, the emphasis on burden sharing among creditors does not necessarily lead to improved outcomes regarding the more important question of burden sharing between debtors and creditors.

In this respect, a key issue is whether a strategy that makes official assistance conditional on private sector participation could succeed in promoting orderly debt workouts with private creditors. The rationale for this strategy is that, if the Fund were to stand aside and refuse to lend to a country under financial stress unless the markets rolled over their claims first, private creditors would be confronted with the prospect of default, which would encourage them to negotiate and reach agreement with the debtor. The main weakness of this strategy is that, if the default is not very costly, creditors will have little incentive for restructuring their claims. On the other hand, if it is costly, the IMF will not be able to stand by and let it happen, since the threat to international financial stability, as well as to the country concerned, would be serious. The insistence on IMF non-intervention would be no more credible than an announcement by a government that it will not intervene to save citizens who have built houses in a flood plain.[9] This dilemma provides a strong case for explicit rules prohibiting the building of houses in flood plains or a "grab race" for assets.[10]

Thus it appears that a credible strategy for involving the private sector in crisis resolution should combine temporary standstills with strict limits on access to Fund resources. Indeed, such a strategy has received increased support in recent years.[11] According to one view, access could be limited by charging penalty rates. However, since such

[9]   For this so-called problem of "the inconsistency of optimal plans", see Kydland and Prescott (1977).
[10]   See Miller and Zhang (1998). The same arguments about the ineffectiveness of official assistance policy in securing private sector involvement in crisis resolution were used in favour of the introduction of collective action clauses in bond contracts in order to facilitate restructuring (Eichengreen and Ruhl, 2000).
[11]   A notable exception to calls for smaller IMF packages is the so-called "*Meltzer Report*" (see International Financial Institutions Advisory Commission, 2000). For a discussion of the debate on IMF crisis lending, see Goldstein (2000).

price-based measures are unlikely to succeed in checking distress borrowing under crisis conditions, quantitative limits will be needed. A recent report by the United States Council on Foreign Relations (CFR) on reform of the international financial architecture argued that the IMF should adhere consistently to normal access limits of 100 per cent of quota annually and 300 per cent on a cumulative basis, and that countries should be able to resort to unilateral standstills when such financing proves inadequate to stabilize markets and their balance of payments. The amounts committed in recent interventions in emerging-market crises, beginning with the one in Mexico in 1995, far exceeded these limits, being in the range of 500 per cent to 1,900 per cent of quota.

However, in setting such access limits, it should be recognized that IMF quotas have lagged behind growth of global output, trade and financial flows, and their current levels may not provide appropriate yardsticks to evaluate the size of IMF packages. According to one estimate, adjusting quotas for the growth in world output and trade since 1945 would require them to be raised by three and nine times, respectively (Fischer, 1999). In an earlier proposal – made in an IMF paper on the eve of the Mexican crisis – to create a short-term financing facility for intervention in financial crises, 300 per cent of quota was considered a possible upper limit (see *TDR 1998*, chap. IV, sect. B.4). Such amounts appear to be more realistic than current normal access limits.

Fund resources are not the only source of rescue packages, and in many cases bailouts rely even more on the money provided by some major creditor countries. This practice has often increased the scope for these countries to pursue their own national interests in the design of rescue packages, including the conditionalities attached to lending. It is highly probable that major creditor countries will continue to act in this manner whenever and wherever they see their interests involved, and some debtor countries may even prefer to strike bilateral deals with them rather than going through multilateral channels. However, limits on access to Fund resources should be observed independently of bilateral lending under crisis. Furthermore, it is desirable to keep such ad hoc bilateral arrangements separate from multilateral lending in order to reduce the scope for undue influence over Fund policies by some of its major shareholders.

A key question is whether such access limits should be exceeded under certain circumstances. For instance, while arguing for strict limits, the CFR report suggested, "In the unusual case in which there appears to be a systemic crisis (that is, a multicountry crisis where failure to intervene threatens the performance of the world economy and where there is widespread failure in the ability of private capital markets to distinguish creditworthy from less creditworthy borrowers), the IMF would return to its 'systemic' backup facilities ..." (CFRTF, 1999: 63). It proposed the creation of a facility to help prevent contagion, to be funded by a one-off allocation of SDRs,[12] which would replace the existing IMF facilities for crisis lending (see box 6).

While the concerns underlying different lending policies for systemic and non-systemic crises may be justified, in practice exceptions to normal lending limits could leave considerable room for large-scale bailout operations and excessive IMF discretion. One possible implication is that countries not considered systemically important could face strict limits in access to Fund resources, but would have the option of imposing unilateral standstills. However, for larger emerging markets bailouts would still be preferred to standstills. Recent events involving defaults by Pakistan and Ecuador (see box 5), but rescue operations for Argentina and Turkey (*TDR 2001*, chap. II), bear this out. In the latter cases, difficulties experienced were largely due to the currency regimes pursued rather than to financial contagion from abroad. However, there is wide concern that if these crises had been allowed to deepen, they could have spread to other emerging markets.

---

[12] In creating this facility all Fund members would agree to donate their share of the allocation to the facility and there would also be agreement that only developing countries would be entitled to draw on the facility. This clearly differs from another proposal, which is to allow the Fund to issue reversible SDRs to itself for use in lender-of-last-resort operations – that is to say, the allocated SDRs would be repurchased when the crisis was over. See Ezekiel (1998); United Nations (1999); and Ahluwalia (1999).

E. VOLUNTARY AND CONTRACTUAL ARRANGEMENTS

As noted above, considerable emphasis is now being placed on voluntary mechanisms for the involvement of the private sector in crisis management and resolution. However, certain features of the external debt of developing countries render it extremely difficult to rely on such mechanisms, particularly for securing rapid debt stand-stills and rollovers. These include a wider dispersion of creditors and debtors and the existence of a larger variety of debt contracts associated with the growing spread and integration of international capital markets, as well as innovations in sourcing foreign capital. As a result, the scope of some of the voluntary mechanisms used in the past has greatly diminished.

Perhaps the most important development, often cited in this context, is the shift from syndicated bank loans to bonds in sovereign borrowing, since, for reasons examined below, bond restructuring is inherently more difficult. Sovereign bond issues were a common practice in the interwar years when emerging markets had relatively easy access to bond markets. During the global financial turmoil of the late 1920s and early 1930s, many of these bond issues ended up in defaults. There was little recourse to bond financing by emerging-market governments prior to the 1990s. The share of bonds in the public and publicly guaranteed long-term debt of developing countries stood at some 6.5 per cent in 1980, but rose rapidly over the past two decades, reaching about 21 per cent in 1990 and almost 50 per cent in 1999 (World Bank, 2000). This ratio is lower for private, non-guaranteed debt, but the increase in the share of bonds in private external debt is equally impressive – from about 1 per cent in 1990 to some 24 per cent in 1999. According to the Institute for International Finance (IIF), from 1992 to 1998, of a total of about $1,400 billion net capital flows to 29 major emerging markets, 23 per cent came from commercial banks and 27 per cent from other private creditors, mainly through bonds (IIF, 1999, table 1).

A second important development is that international lending to emerging markets has been increasingly to private sector borrowers. The share of public and publicly guaranteed debt in the total long-term debt of developing countries exceeded 75 per cent in the 1980s, but

Box 6

RECENT INITIATIVES IN IMF CRISIS LENDING

THE IMF has recently taken steps to strengthen its capacity to provide financing in crises, though this capacity still falls short of that of a genuine international lender of last resort.[1] The Supplemental Reserve Facility (SRF), approved by the IMF's Executive Board in response to the deepening of the East Asian crisis in December 1997, was designed to provide financing without limits to countries experiencing exceptional payments difficulties, but under a highly conditional stand-by or Extended Arrangement (IMF, 1998: 7). However, the SRF depends on the existing resources of the Fund which, recent experience suggests, are likely to be inadequate on their own to meet the costs of large interventions.

The Contingency Credit Line (CCL), created in Spring 1999, is intended to provide a precautionary line of defence in the form of short-term financing which would be available to meet balance-of-payments problems arising from international financial contagion (IMF, 1999). Thus, unlike the SRF, which is available to countries in crisis, the CCL is a preventive measure. Countries can pre-qualify for the CCL if they comply with conditions related to macroeconomic and external financial indicators and with international standards in areas such as transparency, banking supervision and the quality of banks' relations and financing arrangements with the private sector. The pressures on the capital account and international reserves of a qualifying country must result from a sudden loss of confidence amongst investors triggered largely by external factors. Moreover, although no limits on the scale of available funds are specified, like the SRF, the CCL depends on the

---

[1] For a discussion of these facilities, see IMF (2000d). For a discussion of the issues involved in establishing an international lender of last resort, see *TDR 1998* (chap. IV, sect. B.4); and Akyüz and Cornford (1999).

existing resources of the Fund. Originally, it was expected that the precautionary nature of the CCL would restrict the level of actual drawings. However, in the event, no country has applied for this facility. It is suggested that, under the initial terms, countries had no incentive to pre-qualification because fees and interest charges on the CCL were the same as under the SRF. In addition, access was not automatic, but subject to the Board's assessment of policies and risks of contagion effects. The IMF Board took steps in September 2000 to lower charges as well as to allow some automatic access with a view to enhancing the potential use of the CCL (IMF, 2000e), but there appear to be more serious design problems. In particular, countries seem to avoid recourse to it for fear that it will have the effect of a tocsin in international financial markets, thus stifling access to credit.[2]

[2]   For an earlier assessment along these lines, see Akyüz and Cornford (1999: 36). For a more recent assessment, see Goldstein (2000: 12-13).

change offers difficult to implement effectively. Thus, since the Mexican crisis, emerging-market borrowers have been increasingly urged to include so-called collective action clauses (CACs) in bond contracts in order to improve communication with bondholders and facilitate bond restructuring.[14] Such clauses appear to be particularly desirable for sovereign borrowers, who do not benefit from national bankruptcy codes. There are basically three types of CACs:

- *collective representation clauses,* designed to establish a representative forum (e.g., a trustee) for coordinating negotiations between the issuer and bondholders;
- *majority action clauses,* designed to empower a qualified majority (often 75 per cent) of bondholders to agree to a change in payment terms in a manner which is binding on all bondholders, thereby preventing holdouts; and
- *sharing clauses,* designed to ensure that all payments by the debtor are shared among bondholders on a pro-rated basis, and to prevent maverick litigation.

It should be noted that the inclusion of CACs in bond contracts, where allowed by law, is optional – not mandatory – and often depends on market convention. Issuers generally adopt the documentation practices prevailing in the jurisdiction of the governing law. In general, collective representation clauses are not contained in bonds governed by either English law or New York law. Majority action clauses are routinely included in bond contracts governed by English law, but not in those issued under New York law, even though the latter does not preclude them from sovereign issues. Similarly, bonds governed by German and Japanese laws do not generally contain majority action clauses. In these cases, any change to the terms of payment requires a unanimous decision by the bondholders. This is also true for Brady bonds, even when governed by English law. It appears that the inclusion of a unanimity rule was a major reason for the Brady process

---

[14]   See, for example, Group of Ten (1996). This recommendation has been reiterated following the Asian crisis (see Group of Twenty-Two, 1998). For a discussion of problems in bond restructuring and CACs, see Eichengreen and Portes (1995); Dixon and Wall (2000); and Buchheit (1999).

to be implemented through loan-for-bond exchanges rather than through amendments to the existing loan contracts (Buchheit, 1999: 9). Sharing clauses are routinely included in syndicated bank loans, but are uncommon in publicly issued bonds since they are often viewed by markets as a threat to the legal right of creditors to enforce their claims.[15] The absence of sharing clauses, together with the waiver of sovereign immunity, leaves considerable room for bondholders to hold out against restructuring and to enter into a "grab race" for assets through litigation.

According to available data, about one-third of total bonds issued by emerging markets during the 1990s were governed by English law; the share of bonds issued under New York law was lower but still exceeded a quarter, followed by those issued under German law (just under one-fifth) and Japanese law (around 13 per cent). It appears that Asian and particularly Latin American emerging markets have made greater use of New York law than English law in their issues. Japanese law is seldom used in Latin American issues but governs about a quarter of Asian issues, while the opposite is true concerning the use of German law. Between 1995 and 2000, there was an increase in the proportion of bonds governed by New York law, but it is not clear if this is linked to the increased frequency of financial crises in emerging markets (Dixon and Wall, 2000: 145-146; Eichengreen and Mody, 2000a, table 1).

It is estimated that about half of all outstanding international bond issues – including those issued by industrial countries – do not include CACs, and this proportion is even greater for emerging-market bonds. A major concern of emerging markets is that the inclusion of CACs would curtail their access to markets and raise the cost of borrowing because it would signal a greater likelihood of default. They thus insist that such clauses be introduced first in sovereign bonds of industrial countries. Some industrial countries, such as Canada and the United Kingdom, have recently decided to include or extend CACs in their international bond and note issues in order to encourage a wider

---

[15] In the case of English-law bonds issued under a trust deed, the trustee represents the interest of all bondholders and shares any proceeds recovered on a pro rata basis. However, trustees rarely exist for sovereign issues (Yianni, 1999: 79-81; Dixon and Wall, 2000, box 1).

use of such clauses, particularly by emerging markets. International private sector groups find majority voting acceptable, subject to a threshold in the order of 90-95 per cent, but they prefer voluntary exchange offers and are opposed to making CACs mandatory in bond contracts (IMF, 2000b, table 5.2; Dixon and Wall, 2000, table 2).

The empirical evidence on the impact of CACs on the cost of international bond financing is inconclusive (BIS, 1999; Eichengreen and Mody, 2000b; Dixon and Wall, 2000). Indeed, CACs can have two opposite effects. On the one hand, their inclusion can raise the default probability in the eyes of investors since they may create moral hazard for the debtor, leading to a higher risk premium. On the other hand, in the event of a default, such clauses help recover the claims of investors by facilitating bond restructuring. The net effect depends on how CACs affect the perceived default probability and the expected recovery rate. For countries with high credit ratings, the latter effect could dominate, so that the inclusion of CACs may, in fact, lower the cost of bond financing. For lower-rated bonds, however, such clauses may well lead to sharp increases in the perceived risk of default, thereby raising the spread on new issues.

It is not clear if the introduction of CACs in bond contracts could make a major impact on debt restructuring, since experience in this respect is highly limited.[16] In any case, even if such clauses were rapidly introduced by emerging-market borrowers in their new bond issues, the initial impact would be limited because of the existence of a large stock of outstanding bonds without CACs. On the other hand, CACs have been rarely used by emerging markets for bond restructuring even when they are present in bond contracts, partly because of the fear that bondholders' meetings could be used to mobilize opposition against attempts to restructure bonds and to take a decision for acceleration (which typically requires the consent of 25 per cent of bondholders). Clearly, such risks can be serious, since the ultimate decision on restructuring lies with bondholders, and the sovereign debtor does not have the means of obtaining court approval for its restructuring plan, as provided, for instance, under the "cramdown"

---

[16] For some recent experiences of bond restructuring by emerging markets, see box 5.

provisions of the United States Bankruptcy Code for corporate borrowers.

In assessing the potential role of CACs in involving the private sector in crisis resolution, it is important to distinguish between standstills and financial restructuring. The existing practice regarding bond issues leaves little scope for securing a rapid standstill on a voluntary basis.[17] Such a standstill requires representational bodies, such as trustees or bondholder committees, as well as prohibition of litigation by individual bondholders and/or sharing clauses. As already noted, there is strong resistance by private investors to the inclusion of such clauses across almost all jurisdictions, and they are not likely to be introduced on a voluntary basis. Majority action clauses alone cannot secure rapid voluntary standstill and "cramdown" on dissident bondholders, because invoking such clauses is a tedious process and leaves ample time and opportunities for rogue bondholders to impose a financial stranglehold over the debtor.

Private investors often point out that the major financial crises in emerging markets were not precipitated by a rapid exit of holders of sovereign bonds through litigation and a "grab race" for assets, but by short-term hot money (Buchheit, 1999: 7). This is certainly true for East Asia, where sovereign bond debt was generally negligible. However, with the rapid growth of the bond market, granting bondholders unmitigated power of litigation and asset attachment is potentially a serious source of instability. As already discussed, the current emphasis in official lending on private sector participation is unlikely to generate adequate incentives for voluntary standstill and rollover of private debt at times of crisis.

The consequences of unilateral suspension of payments on bonds could be more serious than defaults on bank debt because the effect would be immediately transmitted to secondary markets. A sharp increase in the risk premium and a decline in bond prices would then create considerable opportunities for profit-making by litigious investors (the so-called "vultures"), who could acquire distressed debt at substantial discounts and pursue a "grab race" for assets.[18] On the

---

[17]   This is also recognized by the IMF (2000a: 16).
[18]   The Bulgarian case of 1996-1997 is cited as an example of such market breaks leading to litigations (Miller and Zhang, 1998: 16).

other hand, as some recent bond restructuring exercises show, even when unilateral defaults lead to an agreement on restructuring, the process tends to be disorderly and does not always guarantee significant relief for the debtor (see box 5).

Thus a possible solution would be to combine internationally sanctioned mandatory standstills with majority action clauses in order to prevent a "grab race" for assets and facilitate voluntary restructuring. One proposal (Buiter and Silbert, 1999) favours a contractually-based approach to standstill, which would require all international loan agreements to include an automatic universal debt rollover option with a penalty (UDROP). However, such a clause is unlikely to be introduced voluntarily and would need an international mandate. Another proposal is to empower the Fund to impose or sanction standstills on bondholders at the outbreak of a crisis (see, for example, Miller and Zhang, 1998). This could be combined with IMF lending into arrears, when needed, in order to alleviate the liquidity squeeze on the debtor country and encourage a rapid restructuring. Debt restructuring should be left to a voluntary agreement between the bondholders and the issuer, subject to provisions in the bond contracts. It is neither feasible nor desirable to empower the IMF or any other international authority to impose restructuring of sovereign debt, such as the one practised under the "cramdown" provisions of Chapter 11 of the United States Bankruptcy Code. Nevertheless, the Fund could still exert considerable influence on the process through its policy of conditionality on lending.

It has been argued that proposals such as CACs and standing committees "... are appropriate if it is one's judgement that most countries that experience crises have problems with fundamentals that require debts to be restructured in the absence of a bailout. ...UDROPs and internationally sanctioned standstills are appropriate if one instead believes that most crises are caused by creditor panic, and that all that is required to restore order to financial markets is a cooling-off period" (Eichengreen and Ruhl, 2000: 4, footnote 4). However, the considerations above suggest that both instruments are needed in the arsenal of measures since resolution of most crises requires both a cooling-off period and debt restructuring. Even when the underlying fundamentals are responsible for a crisis, debtors need breathing space, as markets have a tendency to overreact, and this leads to overshooting of asset prices and exchange rates, thereby aggravating the financial difficulties of the debtors. Under such circumstances, standstills would allow time to design and implement cooperative solutions to debt crises.

2. Restructuring bank loans

For the reasons already discussed, it is generally believed that debt workouts are easier for international bank loans than for sovereign bonds, as they allow greater scope for voluntary and concerted mechanisms. Furthermore, the experience in the 1980s with restructuring of syndicated credits, and the more recent negotiations and rollover of bank loans in the Republic of Korea and Brazil, are often cited as successful examples of debt workouts with banks.[19] However, a closer look at these experiences shows that there are considerable weaknesses in the procedures followed, and the outcomes reached appear to bail out – rather than bail in – the private sector.

A main factor which facilitated negotiations with commercial banks in the 1980s was the existence of advisory or steering committees consisting of representatives of banks selected mainly on the basis of their exposure to the debtor country concerned. Clearly, this helped solve the representation problem by providing a forum for negotiations. Furthermore, the presence of sharing clauses in syndicated loan contracts, together with sovereign immunity, deterred litigation against debtor countries. However, agreement required the unanimous consent of committee members, who were also expected to strike a deal that would be acceptable to non-participating banks. This, in effect, allowed considerable room for holdouts by individual banks, in much the same way as bond contracts without majority action clauses. Such holdouts resulted in protracted negotiations, leading to frictions not only between debtors and creditors but also among creditors themselves. As noted by an observer of sovereign debt reschedulings in the 1980s: "From the borrower's perspective, the unanimous consent method translated into always being negotiated down to the minimum common denominator, one acceptable to all members of the commit-

---

[19] See, for example, IMF (1999: 41-42; and 2000b, chap. V); and Eichengreen and Ruhl (2000: 5, footnote 7).

tee based on consultation with their respective constituencies. Namely, one bank had the ability to prevent an entire package from being adopted if it disagreed with any one of its features" (De la Cruz, 2000: 12).

The primary strategy of these negotiations was to avoid default and to ensure that the debtor had enough liquidity to stay current (i.e., to continue servicing its debt). The money needed was provided by the creditor banks as part of the rescheduling process as well as through official lending. In this way banks could keep these assets in their balance sheets without violating regulatory norms regarding credit performance. Maturities were rolled over as they became due, but concessional interest rates and debt cancellation were not among the guiding principles of commercial debt workouts.

Thus, as described in *TDR 1988*, the process involved "concerted lending", whereby each bank rescheduled its loans and contributed new money in proportion to its existing exposure, the aggregate amount being the minimum considered necessary to avoid arrears. The IMF also made its provision of resources to debtor countries – to keep them current on interest payments to commercial banks – contingent upon the banks' making the contributions required of them. Thus, official intervention amounted to using public money to pay creditor banks even though it was designed to bind the banks in. Developing countries saw their debt growing, not only to commercial banks, but also to the official creditors, as they borrowed to remain current on their interest payments (*TDR 1988*, Part One, chap. V).

The negotiated settlements also resulted in the socialization of private debt in developing countries when governments were forced to assume loan losses, thereby in effect shifting the burden to the taxpayers. For example, in the case of Chile, it was noted that "private debts have been included in debt rescheduling being negotiated between the Chilean state and the foreign bank advisory committee for Chile. Apparently the Chilean government caved in under pressure from the bank advisory committee ... To make their viewpoint absolutely clear, foreign banks apparently tightened up their granting of very short-term commercial credits to Chile during the first quarter of 1983, a technique reportedly used with some success 10 years earlier *vis-a-vis* the same country. The International Monetary Fund, also active in the debt rescheduling exercise, has not publicly objected to this threat" (Diaz Alejandro, 1985: 12). For Latin America as a whole, before the outbreak of the crisis in 1982, around two-thirds of the lending by United States banks was to private sector borrowers. In 1983, the first year of debt restructuring, the share of publicly guaranteed debt rose to two-thirds, and eventually reached 85 per cent in 1985 (UNCTC, 1991).

This process of protracted negotiations between banks and debtors, with the intermediation of international financial institutions (a strategy widely described at the time as "muddling through"), continued for several years without making a dent in resolving the problem and removing the debt overhang. Highly-indebted developing countries increasingly questioned the rationale of engaging in such Ponzi financing – whereby they had to keep on borrowing in order to service their debt – which eventually pushed some of them into default on interest payments and led to legal battles with the banks. On the other hand, creditors too became highly sceptical of the merits of "putting good money after bad", and started to dispose of such debt in secondary markets as they accumulated adequate provisions. Through the Brady Plan, the resolution of the crisis eventually involved the private sector, but only after costing the debtors a lost development decade.

In more recent episodes of financial crisis in emerging markets, creditor banks were again able to organize themselves into groups to conduct negotiations with the debtors – with the Republic of Korea in January 1998, and with Brazil in March 1999. Again, in both cases negotiations and agreements came only after the deepening of the crisis. In the case of Brazil, banks were unwilling to roll over debt in late 1998 and agreement was reached only after the collapse of the currency. The government of the Republic of Korea had already suspended payments at the end of December 1997 and, as recognized by the IMF, "... the agreement to stabilize interbank exposure to Korea was struck ... when it was generally recognized that reserves were almost exhausted and that, absent an agreement, a default was inevitable" (IMF, 2000a: footnote 26). A number of banks had already left, which contributed to the turmoil in the foreign exchange market.

While the rescheduling of debt provided some breathing space in both cases, the impact was far less than what could have been achieved with timely standstills. As the government of the Republic of Korea noted in its subsequent report to the G-20, "Many of those who have analyzed Korea's 1997-1998 crisis contend that Korea could have solved its liquidity problems sooner had a standstill mechanism been in place at the time it requested IMF assistance" (Ministry of Finance and Economy, Republic of Korea, 1999: 13), that is, at the end of November 1997.[20] In Indonesia, restructuring came even later than in the Republic of Korea (eight months after the first IMF programme) and made very little impact on stabilizing the economy.[21]

More significantly, such debt restructuring exercises can hardly be portrayed as examples of the private sector bearing the consequences of the risks it had taken. In the restructuring in the Republic of Korea, private debts were effectively nationalized via a government guarantee. This was also the case for subsequent reschedulings by Thailand and Indonesia. Moreover, creditors ended up better after the rescheduling; there was no debt write-off but simply a maturity extension, with new loans carrying higher spreads than the original loans. Although the maturity extension spreads were considered to be relatively low, particularly compared to the IMF's Supplemental Reserve Facility (SRF), such a comparison overlooks the fact that the original bank loans already carried a risk premium.[22]

Problematic as they are, it is found that such restructuring exercises cannot be replicated in many other countries. According to the IMF, "the success of the Korean operation reflected two specific features, which are unlikely to apply to other cases. First, Korea maintained a restrictive capital account regime that forced a high proportion of imported foreign saving to be channelled through domestic banks ... Second, at the onset of the crisis, the sovereign external debt burden was very low. As a result, the extension of a sovereign guarantee ... did not place excessive burden on the sover-

---

[20] For support of this position based on a study of the Malaysian capital controls, see Kaplan and Rodrik (2000, particularly pp. 27-28).
[21] For a description of the East Asian restructuring, see Radelet (1999: 66-67).
[22] The deal included a total debt of $21,740 million owed to 13 banks, and the maturities were extended from one to three years, involving spreads between 225 and 275 basis points. The spread on the SRF was 300 basis points – lower than the maximum spread on maturity extension mentioned in the previous note (Ministry of Finance and Economy, Republic of Korea, 1999: 14).

eign" (IMF, 1999: 41-42). It is thus recognized that debt restructuring with foreign banks can run into serious difficulties when debtors are widely dispersed and the capital account is wide open. The latter feature could indeed discourage creditor banks from entering into restructuring since it would allow other investors to exit at their expense. It is also recognized that a concerted rescheduling of international private bank debt in emerging markets would require sovereign guarantees – a practice inherited, as noted above, from the 1980s – though this is not consistent with the established principles of orderly workouts of private debt.

A further difficulty with such concerted rescheduling operations is that they require the exertion of moral suasion by the supervisory authorities of creditor banks. This gives considerable discretionary power to major industrial countries, which may not apply it in a predictable and equitable manner to different episodes of crisis. As recognized by the IMF, "supervisory authorities are likely to be reluctant to exert moral suasion over the commercial decisions of the banks under their supervision except in the most extreme circumstances, especially in the context of debtors that do not pose a systemic threat to the national or international banking system" (IMF, 1999: 41-42). Again, this means that "non-systemic countries" would have no option but to impose unilateral standstills.

Thus it appears that, for international bank loans, too, there are serious difficulties in reaching orderly and timely workouts on a voluntary and concerted basis in order to stem self-fulfilling debt runs and ensure that the creditors bear the consequences of the risks they take. As in the case of bonds, certain *ex ante* contractual arrangements can help facilitate orderly workouts. One possibility would be to introduce call options in interbank credit lines that would provide an automatic rollover under certain conditions, such as a request for IMF assistance by the debtor country. However, unless all debt contracts incorporate such automatic standstill clauses, including them in interbank lines alone can be counterproductive as it can trigger capital flight as soon as a debtor country runs into financial difficulties and enters into negotiations with the IMF. But such clauses are unlikely to be introduced voluntarily.

F. CONCLUSIONS

It thus appears that an effective and viable strategy for private sector involvement in financial crises in emerging markets would be to combine voluntary mechanisms designed to facilitate debt restructuring with internationally sanctioned temporary standstills to be used when needed. These arrangements need to be accompanied by the provision of international liquidity aimed primarily at helping debtor countries to maintain imports and economic activity, rather than to maintain open capital accounts and allow private creditors and investors to escape the crisis without losses. In general, normal access to IMF facilities, appropriately adjusted to allow for the expansion of world output and trade, should meet such needs. While in some cases additional financing may be required, it should also be recognized that, once exceptions are allowed on grounds of preventing global spillovers and systemic instability, they could easily become the rule, thereby aggravating the moral-hazard problem. In this respect, the minimum strategy should be to require private participation, once official financing is raised above the normal lending limits – or a threshold level – as suggested by some of the Directors at the IMF Board.

Much has been written on the pros and cons of officially sanctioned payment standstills in the resolution of financial crises in emerging markets. There is strong resistance by some major creditor countries as well as private investors to a mandatory temporary stay on creditor litigation on the grounds that it would give rise to debtor moral hazard and weaken market discipline. That this need not be the case has been argued forcefully by the Deputy Governor of the Bank of England:

> Some have argued that articulating a clearer role for standstill may perversely alter debtor incentives, by weakening the presumption that debtors should pay their debts in full and on time. But an orderly standstill process should support, not supplant, market forces and market disciplines. Corporate bankruptcy law grew up as it became clear that market forces delivered losers as well as winners and that some orderly means was needed of dealing with the losers. In this way, bankruptcy law supports the market mechanism.

The situation is no different in a sovereign context. A well-articulated framework for dealing with sovereign liquidity problems should reduce the inefficiencies and inequities of the current unstructured approach to standstills. It would support the international capital market mechanism. It would be no more likely to induce debtors to default than bankruptcy law is to induce corporate debtors to default. (Clementi, 2000)

Another concern is that the threat of a standstill could accelerate capital outflows, thereby aggravating the crisis. Indeed, that is why standstills and exchange controls need to be imposed rapidly, and why the decision to do so should rest with the country concerned. Furthermore, as noted above, the threat of suspension of payments could provide an incentive for creditors to engage in voluntary solutions, particularly for sovereign debt, thereby avoiding the need to impose standstills.

It is also argued that standstills could make it difficult for the debtor country to regain rapid access to international financial markets, forcing it to make painful trade adjustments or to continue to rely on official financing. But that is precisely why such decisions can be expected to be taken with prudence. After all, countries that may need to impose temporary standstills are likely to be those that are closely integrated with international financial markets and would stand to lose if the decision was not exercised with care and prudence. In this respect, the recent Malaysian experience holds some useful lessons. The measures adopted by Malaysia included temporary and selective payments standstills, which sought to prevent the deepening of the currency crisis and widespread insolvencies. There was no significant outflow of capital when the controls were lifted in September 1999, and the country enjoyed an upgrading of its foreign currency credit in December of the same year as well as the normalization of relations with international capital markets.[23]

---

[23] See *TDR 2000*, box 4.1. This situation was also recognized by the IMF: "They [Malaysia's controls] do not appear to have had any significant long-term effect on investor behaviour" (IMF, 2000a, footnote 28). While it is suggested that "capital controls may have contributed to a decline in FDI" compared to the Republic of Korea and Thailand (ibid.: 24), it is quite likely that an important aspect of the stronger recovery of FDI in those two countries in 1999 was the spate of fire-sale investments and takeovers associated with the collapse of asset prices and exchange rates.

There is concern among policy-makers in some emerging-market countries that the inclusion of internationally sanctioned standstills among the arsenal of measures for managing and resolving financial crises and the tying of the provision of large-scale emergency financing to greater involvement of the private sector would limit their access to international capital markets and would also reduce private capital flows to their economies. Such concerns are particularly widespread in middle-income countries with low saving and investment rates and uneven growth performance, and with only limited success in attracting greenfield FDI in tradeable sectors and achieving a stronger export base. Such countries are heavily dependent on financial inflows to meet current-account deficits that tend to increase rapidly as soon as domestic demand picks up.

The measures advocated here will almost certainly somewhat reduce aggregate financial flows to emerging markets by deterring short-term, speculative capital. However, this outcome would have a beneficial side, since such capital flows add little to the financing of development, while provoking significant instability and leading to a stop-go pattern of growth (see *TDR 1999*, chap. V; and *TDR 2000*, chap. IV). In this sense, arguments in favour of such measures have a rationale similar to those in favour of regulation and control of short-term, speculative capital inflows. There is often a temptation for countries to rely on surges in financial inflows, while paying insufficient attention to their longer-term consequences. However, it is difficult to attain rapid and sustained growth without undertaking the reforms needed to address structural and institutional impediments to capital accumulation and productivity growth – reforms which will reduce dependence on financial inflows.

As noted above, the risk of spillovers and contagion to other emerging markets seems to be the main reason for the reluctance of international financial institutions to encourage standstills in countries that are considered important for the stability of the system as a whole. Various channels of contagion have been mentioned in this context, including cutting exposure to other countries, liquidating assets held in other markets in order to meet margin payments, or a general withdrawal of funds from emerging markets (IMF, 2000a: 22). However, the introduction and use of standstills as part of standard tools in crisis intervention would influence investor and creditor behaviour and portfolio decisions, which could result in reducing such potentially destabilizing interdependences. More importantly, as noted above, such orderly debt workout mechanisms are quite different from messy unilateral defaults in their impact on the functioning of international financial markets.

Perhaps one of the most important potential benefits of binding in and bailing in the private sector is the possible impact on policy-making in the major creditor countries. Interest rate and exchange rate policies in these countries exert a significant influence on the competitiveness, balance of payments and capital flows of debtor developing countries, which cannot always be countered with domestic policy adjustment. Indeed, most major financial crises in emerging markets have been associated with sharp swings in exchange rates, interest rates and market liquidity in the major industrial countries. The latter have not always paid attention to the global repercussions of their policies, mainly because adverse spillovers to their financial markets from emerging-market crises have been contained, thanks largely to bailout operations. Nor has the IMF been able to deal with unidirectional impulses resulting from changes in the monetary and exchange rate policies of the United States and other major OECD countries, in large part because of shortcomings in the existing modalities of multilateral surveillance (Akyüz and Cornford, 1999: 31-33). Burden sharing by creditors in emerging-market crises can thus be expected to compel policy-makers in the major industrial countries to pay greater attention to the possible impact of their policies on emerging markets. Indeed, it appears that the potential for adverse spillovers from the crisis in the Russian Federation played a crucial role in the decision of the United States Federal Reserve to lower interest rates in late 1998, even though, on the eve of the Russian default, the Fed was widely expected to move in the opposite direction. As is well known, the default caused considerable losses to Western investors and creditors, and threatened to set a precedent regarding compliance of emerging markets with their external obligations. Thus, it can be expected that effective mechanisms designed to involve the private sector in the resolution of emerging-market crises could bring a greater global discipline to policy-making in the major industrial countries – something that multilateral surveillance has so far failed to achieve.

REFERENCES

Acosta A (2000). Fallacies of the renegotiation of the Ecuadorian external debt. *Focus on Trade*, 56, November.

Ahluwalia MS (1999). The IMF and the World Bank: Are overlapping roles a problem? In: UNCTAD, *International Monetary and Financial Issues for the 1990s*. Vol. XI. United Nations publication, sales no. E.99.II.D.25. New York and Geneva.

Akyüz Y and Cornford A (1999). Capital flows to developing countries and the reform of the international financial system. UNCTAD Discussion Paper, 143. Geneva, November.

BIS (1999). The effects of CACs on sovereign bond spreads. *BIS Quarterly Review*. Basel, Bank for International Settlements, November.

Buchheit LC (1999). Sovereign debtors and their bondholders. UNITAR Training Programmes on Foreign Economic Relations, Document no. 1. Geneva, United Nations.

Buiter W and Silbert A (1999). UDROP: A small contribution to the new international financial architecture. *International Finance*, July.

CFRTF (1999). *Safeguarding Prosperity in a Global Financial System. The Future International Financial Architecture*. Washington, DC, Council on Foreign Relations Independent Task Force, November.

Clementi D (2000). Crisis prevention and resolution – Two aspects of financial stability. *BIS Review*, 11 September.

Das BL (1999). *The World Trade Organization. A Guide to the Framework for International Trade*. Penang, Malaysia, Third World Network.

De la Cruz A (2000). The new international financial architecture. Has 1999 (Ecuador and others) changed anything? Paper presented to the DMFAS Conference on Debt Management, UNCTAD, Geneva, April.

Department of Finance, Canada (1998). Finance Minister announces six-point Canadian plan to deal with global financial turmoil. Press release, 29 September (www.fin.gc.ca/newse98/98-094e.html).

Diaz Alejandro C (1985). Good-bye financial repression, hello financial crash. *Journal of Development Economics*, 19(1/2), September/October.

Dixon L and Wall D (2000). Collective action problems and collective action clauses. *Financial Stability Review*, June.

Eichengreen B and Mody A (2000a). Would collective action clauses raise borrowing costs? NBER Working Paper, 7458, Cambridge, MA, January.

Eichengreen B and Mody A (2000b). Would collective action clauses raise borrowing costs? An update and additional results. Berkeley, University of California, May.

Eichengreen B and Portes R (1995). *What Crises? Orderly Workouts for Sovereign Debtors*. London, Centre for Economic Policy Research.